How Canada Came To Be

A Brief History

By

ANNA JENNINGS STEEN

BAYEUX ARTS
DIGITAL-TRADITIONAL PUBLISHING

HOW CANADA CAME TO BE

CANADA'S EARLY HISTORY FOR YOUNG READERS

(AND OLDER) ❧ CRAFTED BY

ANNA JENNINGS STEEN ❧ WRITTEN IN HONOUR OF THE

ONE HUNDRED AND FIFTIETH ANNIVERSARY OF

CONFEDERATION ❧ THE FIRST DAY

OF JULY ANNO DOMINI

EIGHTEEN HUNDRED AND SIXTY SEVEN

Bayeux Arts, Calgary, Canada

How Canada Came To Be

Published in Canada by
Bayeux Arts Digital - Traditional Publishing
2403, 510 6th Avenue, S.E.
Calgary, Canada T2G 1L7

www.bayeux.com

Book design by Lumina Datamatics

Library and Archives Canada Cataloguing in Publication

Steen, Anna Jennings, author
How Canada came to be / Anna Jennings Steen.

Issued in print and electronic formats.

ISBN 978-1-988440-05-7 (softcover).—ISBN 978-1-988440-06-4 (HTML)

1. Canada—History—Juvenile literature.
I. Title.

FC58.S725 2017 j971 C2017-902653-4 C2017-902654-2

The ongoing publishing activities of Bayeux Arts Digital - Traditional Publishing under its varied imprints are supported by the Canada Council for the Arts, the Government of Alberta, Alberta Multimedia Development Fund, and the Government of Canada through the Book Publishing Industry Development Program.

Printed in Canada
Published: June 2017

Canada Council for the Arts | Conseil des Arts du Canada | Alberta Culture | LIVRES CANADA BOOKS | Canada Government of Canada through the Canada Book Fund

Dedication

For my father
Harry Nelson Jennings
1892 – 1974

Contents

How Canada Came To Be

A Brief History

A lighthouse on the coast of Newfoundland/Labrador, looking east across the Atlantic Ocean

I
Newfoundland

Canada begins in Newfoundland.

Every day begins with the sun rising from the sea and shining first on this land jutting far out into the Atlantic Ocean, the furthest east in North America.

Recorded history in North America also begins in Newfoundland. The first Europeans to land were the Vikings, the great sailors and navigators of the Middle Ages. With their leader, Leif Ericsson, they established a settlement, for a time. But there was not much to keep them in this cold and rocky place, and they soon moved on, leaving behind the remains of their outpost which can still be seen at L'Anse aux Meadows on the coast of Labrador.

That was more than a thousand years ago, in about 1000 AD. It was nearly another five hundred years before the next Europeans landed.

In the space of those five hundred years the world changed. By the end of the 16th century Europe had come out of the Dark Ages and beyond, and was enjoying that glorious binge of learning and inventing and exploring called the Renaissance.

II
Marco Polo

Since before history began people have been curious. This has led people to venture beyond the world they knew into strange lands. Visitor and host might begin by exchanging friendly gifts and pretty soon they had become trading partners.

Stone Age people bartered with people in the next valley. As time went on Egyptians traded with people in east Africa and the eastern Mediterranean; Greeks and Phoenicians traded further into Western Europe. The Romans went further still, throughout the known world and as far west as the British Isles. The Arabs in the Middle Ages had trade routes that went right through the heart of Africa. And so on it went. Once people get used to the good things that trade brings they don't want it to stop.

Marco Polo was born in Venice around 1254. His father and uncle were already doing a brisk trade in the Middle East, travelling overland through Constantinople, and were away from home for years at a time. By 1265 they had expanded their business to the Mongol Empire. They arrived at the summer capital of Shang-tu (known in a famous poem as "Xanadu"). Here they were welcomed by Kublai Khan, grandson of Genghis Khan. He made the Polos his ambassadors to the Pope; he liked to have able foreigners in his employ.

When Marco was just seventeen his father and uncle took him with them on a journey to Asia. They carried with them letters from the Pope's representative in Palestine to the Great Khan. From Acre in Palestine they travelled overland through what are now Turkey and northern Iran to the Persian Gulf, then overland toward the Mongol capital via eastern Iran and Afghanistan. Following the main Silk Road they came to the borders of China and the Mongol capital of Shang-tu. Here they presented their letters and the sacred oil from Jerusalem, as requested, to Kublai Khan.

For the next sixteen or seventeen years the Polos lived and worked in the Emperor's dominions. These included Cathay (north China) and Mangi (south China). They may have moved with the court from the summer residence to the winter one—modern Peking (or Beijing).

Marco was only twenty when he first reached Cathay. He was one of the first Europeans ever to see the fabled winter court of Kublai Khan. The Great Khan himself delighted in Marco's stories of other lands and sent him on fact-finding missions to other parts of the empire. Marco seems to have considered himself an adoptive son of his new country.

Marco Polo wrote a book about his adventures and the strange and fabulous things he had seen, which delighted Europeans and later became the subject of novels, poems and plays. He himself was treated like a movie star. Some people later on accused him of making it all up. There is a story that, when asked on his deathbed to take back the "fables" he had "invented", he replied that he had told barely half of what he actually saw.

The main thing about Marco Polo and his writings is that he got people excited about the exotic East. Because of this a link was established between Europe and the Far East which became the basis for profitable and enduring trade. For the next couple of centuries Europe came to depend on trade with the East—and all this trade was funnelled through Constantinople.

Then came the Arabs, who had been spreading their message of Allah throughout the known world. In 1453 they at last succeeded in capturing Constantinople, and suddenly the world changed. Overnight Constantinople turned from being a Christian capital into a Muslim one. Many scholars and artisans fled westward, bringing their knowledge with them to add to that new flowering of western civilization, the Renaissance.

But the most important thing was that people had to look for another route to the East, by sea.

This is where our story really begins.

Marco Polo departing from Venice

III
John Cabot

It would not have been possible to look for a new route to the Indies, much less to find one, without new technology. In the 15th and 16th centuries shipwrights and sailmakers in Western Europe were building new vessels that could go faster and farther than anything in the East. Before this, sailing ships had to stay fairly near land and wait for favourable winds in order to get where they were going. But this new advance in sailing technology meant that Europeans could now sail *into* the wind and, thus, across the Atlantic. The hunt was on for a North West Passage. This was the beginning of a new age, the Age of Sail.

John Cabot, (Giovanni Caboto), was an Italian navigator sent by King Henry VII of England to seek out new lands and sea routes.

On June 24, 1497, five years after Columbus had sailed to the West Indies, Cabot landed on the rocky coast of Newfoundland and raised a cross and the banner of England to claim the territory for his royal patron. (As well as the English cross of St. George, he also raised the banner of St. Mark, the patron saint of his home town, Venice.)

He and his men followed a trail inland, saw a dead campfire and a carved and painted stick, but no people. They collected fresh water, then got nervous and returned to the ship.

After that the English, for the time being, were too busy with problems at home to launch more voyages of exploration into the New World. They still kept a foothold in the fishing waters off Newfoundland, playing host to sailing ships, including Basque, Spanish and Portuguese, which came to the Grand Banks every year to fish for cod and put in at the port of St. John's.

But the great adventures were yet to come, in the age of Elizabeth.

The capture of Constantinople, 1453

IV
The Age of Elizabeth

much of the 1500's

The 16th century was the great age of sea exploration. Europeans were finding new lands, making maps. Competition for trade and sea power was fierce. It was the height of the Renaissance, a time of excitement, risk and adventure. The men who sailed to new worlds for the first time five hundred years ago were like the men who first blasted into space and walked on the moon in our time, except they sometimes had less idea where they were going, and even less assurance of getting back.

Vasco da Gama had managed to sail east around the Cape of Good Hope to India, giving Portugal a commercial advantage over other Europeans, for the time being. But it was still a very long way to go. What was needed was a route going in the other direction, a northwest passage.

About this time, Columbus stumbled onto the "West Indies" in his quest for a western route to the real Indies, and laid the foundation of a very rich Spanish empire in the Southern Americas. Soon everyone was looking for treasure. Europeans thrilled to tales (some of them true) of fabulous riches to be found in Mexico and further south, of silver and precious stones as common as pebbles, of streets paved with gold.

We think of much of the 1500s as the Elizabethan Age. This was when Queen Elizabeth I of England sent men and ships on great sea ventures. This later led to the establishing of a British North America and, eventually, to the founding of our country.

It was an age of pirates.

Spain and England were at war, the Catholic Spanish attacking the Protestant queen of England. By royal command, English ships called privateers were sent to stop Spanish galleons sailing from Mexico into the Caribbean, and take their cargo of gold, silver and other treasures. Later on, some of these privateer captains went into business, not for the Queen, but for themselves. Then they were called pirates. Other seafarers became explorers and even national heroes.

The most famous seaman of the age was Sir Francis Drake. He started as a privateer and became so well-known for his seamanship that in 1577 he was chosen to lead an expedition into Spanish waters off South America, seeking new territories beyond. With a crew of less than 200 men and five small ships, he succeeded in rounding the tip of South America, and sailed north up the Pacific coast. The Spanish were too surprised to stop him.

He then tried to return to England by sailing up the west coast of North America and through the Northwest Passage, west to east, back to the Atlantic. In doing so he was the first European to see the west coast of Canada. He got as far north as Vancouver; but the cold was too much and he turned back to sail west, into the Indian Ocean, round the Cape of Good Hope and eventually, laden with treasure and spices, back to England and Plymouth harbour. The year was 1580, three years after they had set sail. Drake had become the first captain ever to sail round the world.

Eight years later the Spanish sent a huge attack force of ships to invade England. In 1588 this Spanish Armada was defeated by the English fleet that Elizabeth had built. Drake played a large part in this drama, and his name became legend.

After that Spain's rule on the high seas was over. England, Holland and Portugal now had their chance. Meanwhile, the quest for a better, western route to the Indies continued.

In 1576 another sea captain named Martin Frobisher was commissioned by the Queen to search for the Northwest Passage to the Pacific. (Like Drake, he later played a big part in defeating the Armada). After crossing the North Atlantic he landed in Labrador/Newfoundland—about eighty years after John Cabot. Sailing on up the east coast, he became the first to discover Hudson's Bay. (Henry Hudson came in second, several years later, and gave it his name). While in the eastern Arctic, by the way, Frobisher and his men celebrated the first Thanksgiving in North America, in 1578.

Then along came Sir Humphrey Gilbert looking for—yes—the Northwest Passage. But this time there was another royal commission: to establish a colony. In 1583 Gilbert and his men landed at St. John's, Newfoundland, and claimed it for England and Queen Elizabeth. So Newfoundland became the first English possession in the New World.

Cabot, Frobisher, Gilbert, Hudson; their discoveries formed the basis for early English claims to much of the country that was to become Canada.

But meanwhile, there was another claimant to this land—France.

Queen Elizabeth I

V
Cartier

After Cabot had prepared the way, there were no more British voyages to North America for a long time. But while the British were occupied with matters at home, a new expedition to the new world had been launched, this time by the French.

In 1534 Jacques Cartier was commissioned by the king of France to sail to the New World in the hope of finding a northerly passage to the Orient, or at least some gold. (It's possible he had been this way before in his youth, as a sailor on a fishing vessel to the Grand Banks).

Cartier left St. Malo on the coast of Brittany on April 20th, 1534, arrived at Newfoundland on May 10, then sailed on to Labrador. This was his impression of the rocky, barren land: "I am rather inclined to believe that this is the land God gave to Cain."

Cartier and his men met natives in canoes who signed to them that they wanted to trade. "We likewise made signs to them that we wished them no harm," Cartier wrote in the ship's log. After that they traded knives and other iron goods for skins. But Cartier was more interested in finding that passage to the Orient. He explored the Strait of Belle Isle, then moved westward, where the land was at least more green and fertile than Labrador.

At the Baie de Gaspé Cartier met the St. Lawrence Iroquoians. He presented them with gifts and was introduced to their leader, Donnacona. A celebration followed, which was spoiled somewhat when the Frenchmen put up a thirty foot-high cross engraved with the words "Long Live the King of France". This made the natives a bit uneasy. But they soon became interested in trading again. Donnacona even agreed to let his two sons go back to France with Cartier, in order to fetch more iron goods.

The next year Cartier returned with a third ship and twice as many men as before. Donnacona's sons had told him of a great river, a long route to the interior, which no one had ever explored to the end. Of course Cartier thought this sounded like the passage to the Orient. So he was led to his greatest discovery—the mighty St. Lawrence River.

On their journey up the river Cartier and his men saw many wonders of the New World for the first time: beluga whales, walruses, and many kinds of birds that were new to them. At the village of Hochelaga (today's Montreal) they were met by more than a thousand people who showered them with gifts—fish and food in such quantity that "it seemed to rain bread". There followed much celebration and dancing.

Freeze-up came early that year, and Cartier and his men were forced to build a fort down river for the winter, at a village called Stadacona (now Quebec City). Soon everyone was ill, and many men died. The natives offered the Frenchmen a drink brewed from the white cedar tree. Not long afterwards, as it seemed miraculously, the Frenchmen were well and healthy again. They didn't know it at the time, but they had most likely been cured of scurvy.

After Cartier's third voyage of exploration he returned to France carrying what he thought were the riches the king had sent him to find. But the diamonds turned out to be quartz and the gold was nothing but iron pyrite. Cartier never returned to the New World.

One of Cartier's most lasting discoveries grew out of a misunderstanding. On his second voyage, while they were sailing through the Gulf of St. Lawrence, around Anticosti Island, two native boys pointed and said this was the way to "Kanata". By this they meant the "village", Stadacona, where Donnacona was chief. Cartier took it to mean the whole "province of Canada".

The name seems to have stuck.

Cartier meets the Hochelagans

VI
Champlain

The history of civilization is a history of farmers migrating and moving in to take over the land from hunters. This great change probably began in the Near East about 10,000 years ago, and has continued off and on ever since. Almost the only part of the world where people still live mainly by hunting is in a vast region of northern North America, stretching twenty-five hundred miles across, from eastern Canada to Alaska. When Cartier first came to the New World in the 1500s nearly the whole of North America was a hunting culture. The French were the first permanent European settlers and agriculturalists on the continent. This is the story of how that happened.

By the end of the sixteenth century France was ruined, the result of years and years of religious wars. Even the king was poor. "My shirts are all torn, my doublet has gone through at the elbow, and my soup pot is often upside down", wrote Henry IV. So he set about to rebuild his kingdom. He hoped furs from the New World would do for France what gold from Peru had done for Spain. He decided to found a company for colonizing New France.

The company was given a monopoly over the fur trade, from what is now Philadelphia all the way up to Cape Breton. In exchange for profit from furs, investors in western France were prepared to finance a colony. The man they sent to the New World was a soldier and sailor from Brittany—Samuel de Champlain.

Champlain's father had been a sea captain, and young Samuel learned very early about navigation and warfare. As a member of that first expedition in 1603 he went up the St. Lawrence as far as Tadoussac, then all the way to the Lachine Rapids. On a second expedition, in partnership with

Pierre de Monts, they planned to make a permanent trading post in Acadia (the Maritimes). They decided to winter on the island of Ste. Croix, but the usual terrible weather and an outbreak of scurvy spoiled that. Eventually, after sailing south for a bit, they returned to the Bay of Fundy and there, in 1604, they built the settlement of Port Royal.

Champlain stayed there through the winter, but he soon saw that his men were suffering from winter depression. So, good leader that he was, he invented the Order of Good Cheer. They organized parties and festivities and put on a play called "The Theatre of Neptune in New France". Thus began the first permanent French settlement in Canada.

On another expedition in the spring of 1608 Champlain, (now the Lieutenant General of New France), arrived at Tadoussac in command of a new ship, the "Don de Dieu", (Gift of God). From there he took to the rivers, in a nice light craft designed for the purpose. He passed Ile aux Cadres, Riviere du Geoffrey and Cap Torment, all named by Jacques Cartier. He was as unimpressed by the coast as Cartier had been. But he was delighted when he saw the Ile d'Orléans, calling it "the beginning of the lovely and fine land of the great river". From there he scouted for a worthy site for a settlement.

In July he found it. Not only was this site beautiful, but it had military advantages as well. The cliffs rose almost straight up, high above sea level, and the river at that point was little more than half a mile wide. No invader would have a chance, he thought. Champlain decided to call his colony by its Algonkin name—Quebec.

Work began at once on the buildings and fortifications, including a palisade with platforms and cannons guarding the river. France's enemies soon saw that Champlain was planning to control the river. One day, as Champlain was puttering in his garden, one of his sailors came up to him and whispered that four of Champlain's men had been hired, by the Basques and the Spaniards, to murder him.

That evening Champlain invited the conspirators to come over for a glass of wine. As soon as they arrived they were arrested and thrown into prison. After a brief trial three of them were sent back to France, Champlain remarking that they deserved to hang. The ringleader, Duval, was condemned to death, strangled and decapitated. According to the custom of the time, his head was put on a stake and displayed where everyone at the fort could see it, as a strong reminder about loyalty and duty.

The natives living around the settlement were certainly impressed. Here was a man, they thought, who could be not only a dangerous enemy, but a valuable ally in their wars against the Iroquois, which had already been going for many years. In exchange for this kind of support they could be persuaded to bring their furs to Quebec. Years later Champlain chose, from among several tribes including the Montagnais and the Algonquin, an alliance with the powerful Huron confederation. "I promised to help them in their wars, as much to force them to love us as to assist in my undertakings... which could not succeed without their help", he wrote. In other words, without the native trappers there was no fur trade.

Meanwhile, in the spring of the next year, 1609, Champlain set out on the warpath with three hundred natives and nine Frenchmen. He was looking forward to the chance to explore further into the continent than any European before. Unfortunately most of the party began to get cold feet the further they went within range of the Iroquois, and Champlain was left with only sixty natives and two Frenchmen by his side when finally they faced the Iroquois at Ticonderoga. "The whole night", Champlain wrote, "was spent in dancing and singing," and in hurling insults. Champlain's men warned the Iroquois that "they would see a kind of warfare they had never seen before". They were referring, of course, to that grandaddy of the modern rifle, the arquebus.

At dawn two hundred Iroquois attacked. Champlain signalled to the two remaining Frenchmen waiting in the woods and then moved in front of the natives, his armour glinting in the sun. With just three bullets it was over. The Iroquois were so astonished that two chiefs could be slain even though they wore armour made of cotton thread and wood, proof against arrows, that they panicked and fled.

It was a costly victory, for now the Iroquois united against their new enemies, the French.

The powerful Iroquois confederacy was made up of five nations: the Mohawk, the Oneida, the Onondaga, the Cayuga, and the Senecaa—a truly terrifying war machine. Because the Huron asked him to, Champlain fought the Iroquois in several more encounters. These were the first incidents in a rivalry for control of the fur trade between the Huron and the Iroquois which was to last for a very long time. After losing so many warriors to European fire power, the Iroquois tended to avoid Frenchmen with guns for the next twenty years. They began to realize that they needed European guns if they were to win. They got them, in exchange for furs, from the Dutch who had been trading along the Hudson River.

Champlain now realized that to spread French influence, he would have to learn to travel the continent's waterways. He saw that native know-how was his key to power, so he sent some of his men to live among the Huron and learn all they could from them. One of these was an eighteen-year-old named Etienne Brulé. Champlain was very fond of him and thought of him as a son. After spending the winter months in Huronia learning the native customs, laws and language, Etienne returned, accompanied by two hundred Hurons, and himself dressed like one. He was full of enthusiasm for the things he had seen and the way he had been treated.

Now Champlain wanted to go and see for himself. Arriving in the land of the Huron, he was amazed to find a more complex society than he had imagined. Like their cousins the Iroquois, the Huron were farmers as well as hunters; they grew corn, squash and beans. Champlain wrote of "eighteen villages" with a total of 30,000 souls. Their cabins were covered with bark, with a space to keep corn. In one cabin there was "a place for twelve fires and twenty-four families". The men would go out to other "nations" to "trade and barter for what they lack". Here indeed were most admirable associates and business partners.

Over the next twenty years Champlain was very busy. During that time he made twenty Atlantic crossings, seeking new investors and colonists. At France's insistence he received and sent into the wilderness the first of the missionaries in North America. In 1610 he married Helene Boullé, daughter of the king's lord chamberlain. In 1627 he convinced the most powerful man in France, Cardinal Richelieu, to invest more in the colony. The Company of the One Hundred Associates was founded, and Champlain was made Governor of the colony. He saved and rebuilt the French colony after attempts to occupy or destroy it. And always he laboured over its financing.

One sad and sour note marring his years of success involved the young man he had been so fond of, Etienne Brulé. Brulé made the fatal mistake of trading with the Iroquois. The Huron were furiously angry, and it was said that they tortured, killed and ate him. After this, because they were afraid to face Champlain, they stopped coming to Quebec to trade.

Champlain sent them a message, that they had nothing to fear. No one will ever be sure if he was just thinking of the good of the colony, or if perhaps he too was angry at Brulé's traitorous behaviour.

In the end, though by now Champlain was old and tired, his life's work had paid off. His colony had taken root. A new people, half French and half native, had grown up in this new world, since those early years when he had happily and confidently proclaimed "Our sons shall marry your daughters". In 1635, after winter had set in, Champlain died peacefully in the colony he had founded, fought for and loved—which owed to him its very existence—the city of Quebec.

The Iroqois defeat, 1613, drawn by Champlain himself

VII
Missionaries

During Champlain's time a great upheaval was going on in Europe, one of the biggest happenings in all of European history, and one that was to alter the course of world events forever. This was the Protestant Reformation.

For more than a thousand years before then, nearly all of Western Europe had been Roman Catholic, with the Pope in Rome as head of the Christian Church. But after 1517, when Martin Luther set off this great change in everybody's lives, society was split up into Protestant and Catholic.

The heat was on. There were arguments, family fights, bloody battles and wars. It was partly because of this turmoil that Henry IV, through his agent and ally, Champlain, had been seeking a place in North America for a colony. Both men were sickened by the horrors of years and years of religious wars in France and the cruelties of Frenchmen to each other. Both men believed it was possible to found a new society where all peoples and all religions could live side by side in peace, where society could make a fresh start in a New World.

Meanwhile, competition was fierce between the two sides, and for this reason the Catholic Church began a Counter-Reformation. They did everything they could think of to gain more converts and to spread their influence in the New World as well as the Old. So it was that France sent missionaries to Quebec.

The first three who came to Champlain's growing settlement in 1615 faced a difficult task. The Huron did not seem to take to the Christian god. Friar Gabriel Sagard of the Recollet order wrote: "It is the belief of the Hurons that the Creator is named Yoscaha, and has a grandmother named Ataensiq. That he sows wheat, works, drinks, eats, and sleeps like other men. That all the animals of the world belong to him... They also believe that certain spirits dominate all rivers, voyages, trading, wars, celebrations and sicknesses. They believe that souls are immortal and, on departing the body, go to dance and rejoice."

The main task of bringing Christianity to the natives of New France was taken on by members of the Society of Jesus, also known as the "soldiers of Christ"—the Jesuits. This was a religious order founded by St. Ignatius Loyola in Spain, about the same time that Cartier was making his first voyages to the New World. They were noted for their educational, missionary and charitable works, and had already had much success in other parts of the world.

The thirty thousand Huron, however, were to prove more difficult. They did not welcome Paul Le Jeune and his fellow missionaries, Charles Lalemant and Jean de Brébeuf. Le Jeune soon saw that the Huron would have preferred to receive Frenchmen armed with guns, protection against their enemies the Iroquois, rather than men in long black robes carrying only crosses. The missionaries tried everything, offering presents and promising to help paddle the canoes, but the Huron were not interested.

Life among the Huron was not easy for the missionaries. It was unlike anything they were used to: no tables or household furnishings of any kind, eating and sleeping on the ground, drinking out of cups made of bark. They had no salt or bread or wine (except what was kept for celebrating the mass). Nor did they have much success. One native shaman claimed the Christian God did not live in Canada, that native souls might be different from European ones, that they went to a different place after death.

Still the missionaries refused to give up. Gradually some natives started to respond, and as time wore on some became Christians. One Christmas, in about 1643, Jean de Brébeuf wrote a Christmas carol, in the Huron language, telling in a new way the story of Christ's birth. In some parts of the world it has become known as the "Canadian Carol". We call it the Huron Carol.

Paul Le Jeune, who had become the superior of the Jesuits of Quebec, kept a diary of what life was like in Huronia. This diary, and the writings of other Jesuits, were eventually published as "Relations of the most remarkable events that have occurred during the mission of the Fathers of the

Company of Jesus in New France". Much of our knowledge of that time is owing to these "Jesuit Relations". Translated into Latin, Italian and German, they stirred great interest among readers in Europe.

So much interest, indeed, that a group of Catholic idealists in France were inspired to found a colony in the New World. They dreamed of bringing Christianized natives together with Frenchmen to create a new Kingdom of God. Many people tried to discourage them. Because of war with the Iroquois and their constant raids, they said, the scheme was "absurd", foolish and dangerous.

But danger never deterred the true believer. These people may have been foolhardy but they were also very brave, and in 1642, under the command of a soldier named Maisonneuve, the Christian village of Ville Marie was founded, by volunteers, on the island of Montreal. Unfortunately it did not last; after ten years most of the people in the colony were forced to give up and go home. But there remains, today, the modern great city of Montreal; and somewhere near the city's centre there is a large and beautiful public "square" called Place Ville Marie.

Tragically, Huronia did not fare as well. Little was understood in the early seventeenth century about how diseases are transmitted, and even less was known about immunization. For thousands of years the people of North America had lived isolated from the rest of the world, and had no resistance to the diseases brought by Europeans. Influenza, measles and smallpox brought by Jesuits and fur traders swept like wildfire through the Huron population. Mother Marie de l'Incarnation, who came from France to found the first Ursuline convent in Quebec in 1641, wrote an account of this time. An old Huron woman said to her: "The black robes are casting spells on us and making us die. They came into a village where everyone was doing just fine: as soon as they arrived, everyone died... It is only the places where they never set foot that have been spared illness and death".

The Iroquois, who had vowed to get rid of the Huron in order to take over as middlemen in the fur trade to Montreal, now had their chance. Illness had weakened the Huron, and in 1649 the Iroquois attacked. They massacred the Huron, who had no guns; the French had refused to sell to them. They then turned on the missionaries, including the Jesuits—Jogues, Lalemant and Brébeuf—who were taken prisoner, tortured and killed.

The Iroquois then destroyed Huronia. Of the thirty thousand Huron, only a few thousand survived: some were adopted by the Iroquois, some resettled in the west, and some went to live on the Ile d'Orléans under the protection of the cannons at Quebec. The French were devastated, for they were seeing the last, not only of the powerful Huron nation, but of their most valued trading partners and friends. In the words of Father Le Jeune, "This people has been wiped off the face of the earth".

But they had not seen the last of the Iroquois.

Father Brébeuf

A Pioneer missionary

Iroquois - "fearsome"

VIII
The Rise of New France
Part 1

During the 17th century the Iroquois were a fearsome military power. They not only destroyed the Huron nation, but before that they had battled the Mohican and gained control of the whole Hudson valley. Now they turned their attention to New France.

The little French colony numbered altogether about 350. The 12,000 strong Iroquois nation could at any time call up more than 2,000 soldiers. They were best at guerilla warfare, meaning they would strike suddenly out of nowhere and as quickly disappear, along with their captives. The "Jesuit Relations" describes an Iroquois raid: "They come like foxes in the woods. They attack like lions. They flee like birds."

Beginning in 1643 the Iroquois attacked Ville Marie and Trois Rivières, and for the next twenty years the colony was in a state of siege. This meant that the entire fur trade was shut down: the French could not go out to other tribes to trade, and other tribes could not come in to them. Agriculture was disrupted. A farmer might go out in the morning to work the land and never be seen again alive. No one could hunt or fish or plough or clear land without risking his life. Most of the livestock had been killed and there was not a single horse left in New France.

Ten percent of the population had been killed in Iroquois raids, and many captives were tortured. One group of sixteen French traders who tried leaving the fort, to protect a load of furs travelling down the Ottawa River, were massacred, except for five prisoners who were eaten. (Symbolically, that is: usually a bite was taken from the heart to gain the enemy's courage, so it was really a sign of respect!) Throughout all this the Government of France, being too busy with other matters, refused to help. The situation was desperate.

Just when it seemed the colony could go on no longer, two things happened. The uncaring and disinterested prime minister of France died, and Louis XIV was crowned King. Louis was only twenty-two, but he dreamed great dreams of empire, and the last thing he wanted was to start his reign by losing New France. So he set out to put things right.

The first thing he did was to change the colony's status as a private commercial enterprise, and make it like any other province of France, with a governor and an intendant.

The King's next move was to do something about the Iroquois. In June of 1665 the colonists were surprised to see four ships arrive at Quebec carrying several companies of France's best soldiers. At the same time came the first governor, de Courcelle; the commander of the troops, de Tracy; and the colony's first intendant, Jean Talon. Later that same year came an even greater surprise—a shipload of horses. These were much admired by the natives, who had never seen horses before and wondered how these "French moose" could be so gentle and easy to handle.

At first the military was hampered by lack of equipment; they set to work building forts but they had no tools, no carpenter among them, and no proper clothing or shoes. Worse, de Courcelle was too impatient to wait for native guides or military advice. Without any experience of Canadian winter he decided to attack the Iroquois at once, in their own territory, in January. Of course it ended badly. They were so ill-prepared, they had "no snowshoes... few axes... only one pair of moccasins and one pair of socks" among them. The expedition, instead of punishing the Iroquois, killed half its own soldiers because they got lost and froze to death. The remaining soldiers survived only through the kindness of the English at the little post of Schenectady, where the English had just replaced the Dutch.

Apart from this bad beginning, however, the French under the regimental command of de Tracy were more successful. Eventually the Iroquois, already suffering from smallpox, began to see they could not win against this new French military strength, and they made peace.

New France was now ready to enter into a new and prosperous age. In New France, unlike in France, there was plenty of work to be had and anyone—farmers, soldiers, labourers—if they worked hard could eventually become quite rich. Many of the soldiers chose to stay and accept the king's offer of land and money; some of the officers were made seigneurs and received an income from their tenant farmers. All of them were about to become the fore-fathers of a new nation. The only trouble was a lack of women. Colbert, the king's minister, realized that more people were needed for New France to grow bigger and stronger. The presence of so many soldiers meant that the population was mostly male.

The solution was simple. In October of the same year (1665) more ships arrived carrying, not soldiers, not horses, but the first of hundreds and hundreds of women—"les filles du Roi". They had been chosen and sent by the King to find husbands and help build up the population of New France. Some were orphans, some had run away from bad homes. All of them were poor, and their only hope for a new start and a decent future was New France. According to Marie de l'Incarnation, who sheltered many of these young women until they could get settled, almost all of them were well provided with a dowry given by the King. If any of them had a bad attitude they were sent back. Jean Talon saw to it that married couples were rewarded with more money the more children they had. He also ordered that "all boys who marry at twenty or less, and all girls at sixteen or less, will receive 20 livres on their wedding day."

The plan worked. By 1670 the colony had grown to almost 10,000 and counting. These colonists were tough and hard-working. Whether they had been soldiers, or penniless girls, or indentured servants, they all eventually prospered and became a proud new race of people. They did not like to be referred to as "peasants"—they were "Habitants".

1670

IX
The Rise of New France
Part 2

It was about this time (1670) that merchants began to venture further west into the interior of the continent, looking for new tribes to trade with. Hundreds of Frenchmen left the colony for the "Pays d'en Haut", (the area around the Great Lakes), and a new breed of trader, the "coureur des bois", came into being. These men lived in the woods, were wild and independent, recognized no law, and were generally not too well behaved. But they did help to open up a continent.

Jean Talon, who dreamed of a great French empire in America, started this push for more territory, in spite of warnings that New France would get too big for its relatively small population to defend. It had begun as a very small colony, but in the space of about twenty years French explorers claimed land from one end of the continent to the other—from Hudson Bay to the Gulf of Mexico—and explored the Mississippi River. Most of this was against the express wishes of the King. It would also become a great irritation to the English colonies nearby. (In 1670 New France had barely 10 thousand people; the English colonies had 100 thousand.)

Even so the new governor, the Comte de Frontenac, joined in this enthusiasm for more territory, and a new time of trouble began. He formed a partnership with de La Salle, a failed priest who sold cheap alcohol to the natives in exchange for furs worth a hundred times more. This made enemies of Montreal merchants, and did great harm to the natives who were not used to alcohol.

La Salle was obsessed with glory: he wanted to be The Discoverer of a southern sea route to China. In the fall of 1679 he began a series of expeditions on the Mississippi, which had already been partly explored by Louis Joliet and Father Jacques Marquette. During the next four years he got lost, abused his men, and stirred up trouble between native tribes. But he eventually had his way. In April of 1682 he claimed "Louisiana" on the Gulf of Mexico for the King of France.

Louis himself was unimpressed. He saw no use in this territory and frowned on any such enterprises in the future. So La Salle made up a false map to persuade the King that this would be a perfect base from which to attack the Spanish to the south. The King, knowing no better, then made La Salle commander of the whole territory.

From there La Salle continued exploring, but got lost and wandered for two years, without maps, in the marshes of the Mississippi Delta. Some of his men died, the rest revolted. Finally they had had enough; this ruthless, unlovable leader had pushed them too far. One morning in 1687 five of them got together, drew lots, and one of them shot La Salle through the head.

By now Frontenac's overly ambitious policies had wasted France's resources, spoiled native friendships, upset merchants and alienated the Church. Louis XIV could stand it no longer and called Frontenac back to France.

But the French had already become an annoyance to the English colonies as well. The governor of New York in the 1680s remarked that "wherever a Frenchman goes forth in America, it becomes part of Canada". He set out to turn the Iroquois against the French. The Iroquois, as always, wanted to control the fur trade, this time by taking their furs to the English in New York, rather than the French in Montreal. The French were now trading with the tribes to the west, who wanted the French to wipe out the Iroquois. The French allied themselves with the natives by turning them against the English. A complicated web was woven of alliances and betrayals, plots and counter-plots. It was an explosive situation.

To complicate matters further, in the spring of 1689 war had broken out in Europe between France and England. The governor of New York gleefully told this to their allies, the Iroquois. But the "Canadiens" in New France were as yet unaware of the news. Worse, the colony was not fortified, nor was the militia trained, because Frontenac had convinced the King that the Iroquois were not a threat.

At dawn, August 5th, 1689, 1500 Iroquois warriors attacked the village of Lachine. In all nearly 100 French, including women and children, were killed or taken prisoner, and most of the houses were burned to the ground. Unspeakable horrors were committed. Afterwards a number of children were taken away and adopted by the Iroquois. Altogether 42 inhabitants of Lachine disappeared.

News of the war between France and England finally came to the colonists in the autumn of that year, along with a new governor—Frontenac (again)—now a decade older. He, of course, was eager to attack New York at once, but winter was closing in. The Iroquois went on harassing French outposts, until Frontenac decided to act. On February 14th, 1690, he sent militia men and some native allies to attack the English. There was another brutal massacre, this time at the village of Schenectady. In October the English colonists replied by sending a fleet of 34 ships from Boston to the St. Lawrence. Once again Quebec was under siege. This time, though, there were 3000 militia men to defend it, and those cannon up on the cliffs did great damage to the English ships. The English left off after a week, weakened from smallpox and afraid of getting stuck in the ice as winter approached.

As for the Iroquois, they too were exhausted from war and smallpox epidemics, and at last called a halt to the fighting. They wanted a real peace, guaranteed by the French, whom they had learned to respect and trust during a century of French diplomacy, ever since Champlain. In the summer of 1701, with great ceremony and according to Iroquois ritual, 1300 native delegates from more than 40 tribes met in Montreal. There were long speeches, (one by the great Huron chief and friend of Frontenac, Kondiaronk); a ceremony honouring the dead; exchanges of prisoners and gifts. On August 4 the treaty was signed, putting an end to nearly 100 years of war between the French and the Iroquois confederacy. This was the Peace of Montreal, the Great Peace.

X
The 'Golden Age' of New France

The century that began with the signing of the Great Peace promised to be very different from the first century of New France. England and France were again fighting it out in the War of the Spanish Succession, but this time, in North America at least, the French were winning. For a start, although the English colonies had more then ten times the French population, the Iroquois remained neutral and were no longer in the game. Not only that, but the English were afraid of the "Canadien" soldiers, the tough, homegrown "Habitant" variety.

The most famous of these was Pierre le Moyne d'Iberville. He was the first "Canadien" to be made a Chevalier of the Order of St. Louis, the highest military distinction in France. D'Iberville's father, Charles, had come to Canada as a fifteen-year-old servant to the Jesuits. When he died forty-four years later he was a seigneur and one of the richest merchants in Montreal. The son, Pierre, won victories against the English all over the continent, first at Hudson Bay, then at Newfoundland—thus depriving them of their cod fisheries. The people there resisted at first, but changed their minds after d'Iberville burned down St. John's and had a prisoner publicly scalped.

In 1701 Louis IV commanded d'Iberville to found a post at the mouth of the Mississippi, to prevent the English from expanding any further and taking over the whole continent. Seventeen years later this post became New Orleans.

French colonists may have been winning in North America, but in Europe they were just being used as pawns in a political game, to be traded for bigger prizes. In 1713 the War of the Spanish Succession ended and the Treaty of Utrecht was signed. Louis gained the throne of Spain for Philippe of Anjou, thus adding to his own power and influence; but in exchange he had to give away a large piece of his New World empire. By this treaty France returned to Great Britain "the Bay and Strait of Hudson, all of Acadia, as well as the island of Newfoundland." France kept the island of Ile Royale (Cape Breton) and all the other islands in the Gulf of St. Lawrence. Having given up Acadia and Newfoundland, France now had only one access to the all-important Atlantic fisheries—Ile Royale. Since the Grand Banks were essential to their survival, the French decided to beef up the fortification of their one remaining possession on the Atlantic. In 1720 they built there the largest military fortress in all of North America—Louisbourg.

In the meantime New France continued to grow and prosper. By the middle of the century there were 50,000 people, most of them better off and more self-sufficient than they would have been living in France at that time. A typical Habitant family would have a few cows, pigs and chickens, a couple of horses, a pair of oxen for ploughing, and a small flock of sheep for wool. They grew wheat on land which would also have pasture and trees for firewood. They never had to go hungry, because if ever the farm failed to produce, they could always go hunting, fishing and fur trading. There were farms on both sides of the St. Lawrence and Richelieu rivers, running away into the forest in long narrow strips. These were owned by the seigneurs and granted to farmers in exchange for rent and services.

The worst enemy now was, of course, the climate, but after a few generations the colonists began to get the hang of it, even using winter to their advantage. They learned how to use the cold to conserve food; they built houses that could stand up to freezing and thawing; they learned to make clothes that were warm enough; and from the natives they learned the art of travelling on snow shoes. In time winter became fun, so much so that the authorities issued a decree banning sledding and skating in the streets. There followed other rulings with varying penalties and fines for offenders, one banning people from gathering "for the purpose of making snowballs and throwing them at each other". Racing horse-drawn sleighs and carriages through the streets and smashing into people was definitely frowned upon.

New France already had well established social services. Hospitals had been started and continued to be run by women's religious communities; the earliest was way back in Port Royal a century before. Convents run by nuns also provided refuge and help, especially to young women. The Jesuits already had a college in Quebec, the first in North America, where they taught the same curriculum as in France.

Life in New France was becoming more urban and sophisticated. The rising local aristocracy were more and more living the same kind of life as their counterparts in France. This was the beginning of a growing cultural, artistic and social life. There were balls and parties, and everyone was learning to dance. Quebec was becoming quite the glittering little Versailles, and many inhabitants were over-sensitive to the comments of strangers who might think otherwise. Indeed one lady, the widow of a governor, who had been born in Montreal but still hated the long winters and had heard how much better things were in the mother country, made a trip to France. She found it to be quite the contrary. "In truth," she wrote, "if I had been fool enough to believe it, I would have been very much mistaken, because I find nothing [in France] is better than in Canada, except in December, January and February; all the rest is worse."

All in all, this did seem to be the flowering of a Golden Age for this new, small country in a vast new world. But could it last?

Port Royal Hospital

XI
Acadia

Acadia was the earliest of the colonies in New France. It was probably named after the garden of the gods in Greek myth—Arcadia. Certainly it was a kind of paradise: it had perhaps the richest soil in North America, no epidemics of disease, and peaceful harmony. The French lived happily with the local Mi'kmaq, as their allies, and sometimes their relatives by marriage.

There had been settlers in Acadia ever since Port Royal was founded in the early 1600s. But it was their misfortune to be perched on the border between two mortal enemies. So while they were quietly going about the business of farming, the very ground under their feet was being handed back and forth between England and France, the result of continuing wars in Europe. This happened no fewer than six times in less than a hundred years.

The problem for the Acadians was their loyalty to France. In 1713 when Acadia was finally handed over to England, there were about 2,000 French Catholic farmers living there who, naturally, wanted to stay put. Their new sovereign, the Protestant king of England, just as naturally wanted them to swear an oath of loyalty to Great Britain. The Acadians refused. They said that when they had lived under English rule before they had never been asked to swear such an oath. In any case, there were not enough Englishmen on hand to force the issue, and many of them felt that if the French were gone it would be hard for English families to be supported and protected from harassment by the Indians.

Five years later the English again demanded an oath of allegiance. This time the Acadians of Beaubassin, Grand-Pré and Port Royal asked for help from the king of France, through the governor of Louisbourg.

They explained that they could neither take the oath nor leave the country. Clearly they were in an impossible position. But so was the government in London, who feared the Acadians would always be difficult and a danger to the English colonies, and could see no way out other than removing them.

Nothing happened for ten years. Then in 1750 the French were persuaded to sign an oath of loyalty to the British Crown, provided they would never be asked to bear arms in a British war against the French or the natives, and so long as they promised never to bear arms against the British. Four thousand Acadians signed the oath—although the "bearing arms" part was only added in the margin of the document. Now they felt safe. The English now called these new citizens "French neutrals".

By now the Acadian population had doubled, and Louisbourg was considered a threat to business in Boston. The governor of Massachusetts led an expedition to capture Louisbourg, angering the French. Three years later England returned Louisbourg to the French, angering the Bostonians. Four years later, in 1749, the English built their own fortress, Halifax. The boundaries between Acadia and English territory had never been made very clear: France thought the English had just a strip along the coast; the English thought they had everything south of the St. Lawrence. Officially the two countries were at peace, but unofficially the French didn't mind at all if the Mi'kmaq went about being a nuisance to the English, sometimes even cutting their throats. All things considered, it was only a matter of time before things blew up.

The Acadians went on thinking themselves safe and "neutral". But the English colonies were hatching other plans. Not only did they see the Acadians as a threat, they also thought it would be nice to have their land, some of the finest agricultural land in North America.

In July of 1755 the new English governor demanded the Acadians take a new oath, this time without any special conditions. The clause about not having to bear arms had disappeared. Not surprisingly the Acadians refused. No more surprisingly, the Governor decided enough was enough. He decided to expel the Acadians. In August all the French males, from ten-year-old boys to the oldest old men, were gathered together in the church at Grand-Pré to hear the announcement:

"Your lands and tenements, cattle of all kinds and livestock of all sorts are forfeited to the Crown with all other your effects, saving your money and household goods, and you yourselves to be removed from this province."

By now, since the Treaty of Utrecht, Acadia had been British for 42 years and almost all the inhabitants had been born British subjects. In that year of 1755 there were 12,000 Acadians of French origin. The expulsion took five years; at the end of it 10,000 Acadians had gone.

The operation was overseen by Lieutenant Colonel Winslow of Massachusetts. A doctor under his command recorded this exodus in his journal, including details of weather, the burning of houses and barns, and the rounding up of livestock. "We have started moving the inhabitants out", he wrote. "The women were very distressed, carrying their newborns in their arms; others brought along in carts their infirm parents and their personal effects. In short, it was a scene in which confusion was mixed with despair and desolation."

Most of the Acadians went to the American colonies, where they were not wanted. In a world still divided and suspicious as a result of the Reformation and the ensuing Counter-Reformation, the Catholic French did not mix well with the Protestant English. They were at best ignored. One third of them died of typhoid and smallpox. Another third settled in Louisiana. The rest were scattered, mainly over the French and English-speaking world. At the end, fewer than a thousand French people were left in Acadia.

This was the beginning of the end of New France. The end was to come a few years later.

XII
The Seven Years War

By the mid 1700s France claimed most of the North American continent. The inhabitants numbered only about 60,000 people altogether, including Quebec, Louisbourg, villages along the St. Lawrence, and forts in the interior. But alliances with natives helped them control the west, from (Fort) Detroit all the way south to Louisiana.

The English colonies, from Halifax south to Savannah (Georgia), had far more people but far less territory. The Allegheny Mountains barred their way and kept them from expanding further west.

The natives, two hundred tribes of them, lived between these two groups, changing loyalties from time to time. For a long time they had also been divided among themselves. Most sided with the French.

Officially, during this time, there was peace between France and England, in spite of fights and skirmishes, and even that famous shifting of a whole population from Acadia. But these events were merely a warm-up, the prelude to a real war. This was to be the great contest between France and England, and at the end the winner would control all of North America.

Finally, in 1756, war was declared between France and England. This would become a global war, the first one ever, and would come to be called the Seven Years War.

For France, Quebec was the North American centre of operations. In 1756 it became a wartime city filled with soldiers and refugees. The commander-in-chief of the army was the governor general of New France, the Marquis de Vaudreuil, a big, strapping man, born in New France. The commander of the ground troops was the Marquis de Montcalm, an aristocrat and career soldier sent from France. He was short, impatient and vain. The two men did NOT get along, and wrote letters back to France complaining about each other.

The two men weren't just different in size and temperament, they also had very different ideas about how to conduct a war. Montcalm favoured traditional European methods using large orderly forces on a battlefield; Vaudreuil was for the guerilla tactics of the New World, learned mainly from the natives. (It was these tactics, along with native alliances, that would be largely responsible for the French being successful in the interior; that is, until the British sent in the navy.)

Montcalm's aide-de-camp, Bougainville, saw that Indian methods were useful and necessary, and he kept a journal in which he wrote: "They see in the tracks the number that have passed, whether they are Indians or Europeans, if the tracks are fresh or old, if they are of healthy or of sick people, dragging feet or hurrying ones, marks of sticks used as supports. It is rare that they are deceived or mistaken. They follow their prey for one hundred, two hundred, six hundred leagues with a sureness which never leads them astray."

Occasionally the French and English united against the natives when they saw what they thought was un-called-for native savagery. They feared such behaviour, if allowed, would undermine the more "gentlemanly" European methods of warfare. Once, when the British had surrendered Fort William Henry to the French, the natives thought they might help themselves to the spoils of war, and began to strip and massacre the English soldiers. Montcalm and some of his officers, alerted, leaped in and rescued 400 of the Englishmen, risking their own lives in the process. Not only that, they took the Englishmen away from the Indians, shared with them whatever spare clothes they had, and even paid the ransom for some of the Indians' prisoners.

At this stage the French had the upper hand in the war, but the people in the colony were starving, and beginning to wonder if it was all worth it. In France, the French writer Voltaire expressed this in his novel, *Candide*, wondering if it was worth fighting over "a few acres of snow".

But the French were still winning in Europe. The government in England thought that, if they couldn't beat the French in Europe, it would be wise to put more effort into the war in North America. They decided to send a huge force of ships and troops to capture that symbol of French power in North America, the fortress of Louisbourg.

The campaign began, according to old-fashioned European rules of decorum, with an exchange of gifts. The British commander, General Amherst, sent two pineapples to the wife of the French governor; the governor replied by sending the British commander several bottles of champagne. Then the battle began. After a siege and bombardment lasting two months, food and armaments were running low, women and children were suffering, the hospital was destroyed, and half the walls of the fortress were rubble. It seemed to the French governor there was only one reasonable thing to do. He held out long enough to act as a decoy for the British ships and keep them from moving on to Quebec until it was nearly winter and too late in the season, then he surrendered. It was the first real British victory in three years, and the first of more to come.

One of the British soldiers at Louisbourg was thirty-one-year-old Brigadier-General James Wolfe. He had managed to land troops on Ile Royale in a dangerous and rocky place where the French thought it was impossible. He soon gained a reputation for doing daring, reckless things—with success. For this reason he would later be chosen to lead another assault on a dangerous and rocky place: Quebec.

He was not very heroic-*looking*. He was not handsome, nor strong, but thin, humourless, nervous and insecure, and socially awkward. He suffered also from rheumatism and other illnesses, and was convinced he would die young. His unusual behaviour on social occasions, (like getting up for a bit of make-believe sword play in the middle of a dinner party), made some people think he was as mad as a dog with rabies. "Mad, is he?" said George II, King of England. "Then I hope he will bite some of my generals".

In the late spring of 1759 the British sent to Canada an enormous fleet: 29 ships each carrying 800 people; 22 frigates, 80 transport ships, as well as 53 smaller boats carrying 15,000 soldiers, 2,000 cannon, (plus 40,000 cannon balls), and various surgeons, priests and livestock. It amounted to a quarter of the entire British navy. The number of people it carried on board was greater than the population of Quebec at that time, and the fleet stretched like a floating city for nearly 100 miles up the St. Lawrence, farther than the eye could see.

As they sailed up the river, small villages and farms on both shores began evacuating to a safer distance, taking their belongings in carts and escorted by armed guards. Now and then shots rang out as farm boys and old men fired at the ships from the forest along the river. At night the dark was pierced by the many signal fires high up on the cliffs.

On June 27th Wolfe's fleet landed at Ile d'Orléans, and for the first time he saw how high were the walls of the great fortress of Quebec, how steep were the cliffs, and how well defended they were, even for several miles along the north shore. He saw at once that his original plans for taking Quebec would have to be scrapped.

Montcalm tried to halt the British advance by ramming their ships with a small armada of boats set to explode into flames, but their timing was off and the trick was botched. The boats made a marvellous fireworks display before burning themselves out, and the British ships were left unharmed.

Then he appealed to France for more troops, but the government of France was distracted, and sent him only 400 men, most of them sick with fever.

On the eve of one of the great battles of history, both generals, Montcalm and Wolfe, were feeling a sense of doom.

XIII
The Battle for Quebec

Quebec by this time was a sophisticated urban centre, more than 150 years old. A colonial version of the mother country, it had grand architecture, and an aristocracy both elegant and corrupt. It also had a population of citizens who were already proud fifth-generation "Canadiens", and beginning to feel hostile to France because of its indifference to the colonies, and its administrators' treatment of the people, many of whom were near starvation.

The people who struggled to hold everything together and keep up morale were the nuns. They were the nurses, teachers and social workers of the community, even becoming skilled in trades and business. In the days to come, they would turn out to be the city's most valuable citizens.

The battle for Quebec began with a siege. On the evening of July 12th a rocket went up signalling the start of the assault. This was followed by fire bombs made of baskets of pitch, and cannon and mortar fire which smashed walls and destroyed many houses, businesses and warehouses. This was followed by cannon and mortar fire and fire bombs made of baskets of pitch which smashed walls and destroyed many house, businesses and warehouses. A month later a fire started which burned several churches. More than half the town was in ruins, and food was running out. Wolfe thought if he starved out the French the British would win without any more bloodshed. Montcalm thought if they just endured long enough, the French would win. It was a stalemate, with by this time only four weeks to go before winter set in.

Wolfe, feeling sicker and more despondent, feared the disgrace of going back to London with the world's most powerful navy, having accomplished nothing. He wandered up the river, looking at the cliffs and pondering. An idea came to him. Immediately he cancelled all other plans and instead landed troops at a seemingly impossible spot. The French were waiting and expecting the British to land elsewhere, never dreaming of what was to happen next.

At midnight on September 12th Wolfe and a few hundred men landed at l'Anse au Foulon. They spent the next six hours very quietly climbing up an almost hidden goat path which went straight up the cliff for 150 feet. At the top, they overpowered the very surprised French sentries, and there they stood, at dawn, on the Plains of Abraham.

Montcalm and his men, meanwhile, had been up all night guarding a different spot, an hour's march away from Quebec, where they thought the English might land. By now they were very sleepy.

Bougainville was waiting in another likely landing place farther up river, three hours away.

When the unbelievable news reached them, both commanders started marching with their troops toward Quebec. At the same time, Wolfe's men were assembling for battle on the Plains.

The British force consisted of Scots Catholics, kilted Highlanders, Irish farmers and unemployed Englishmen. They were to face a French force of French soldiers, half starved and sleep-deprived, "Canadien" militiamen, and Iroquois and Algonkin warriors.

Montcalm thought there must be another much larger number of British troops somewhere out of sight, so he felt he must act quickly. Without waiting for the other French forces to join him, he marched his men onto the field and ordered them into battle formation. Had he waited for Bougainville and his troops, or even done nothing at all, the outcome might have been different.

Nevertheless the two armies, both unprepared, moved toward each other, and a very disorganized and bloody battle began. The wounded were taken to the nuns' hospital. As one of the nuns recorded: "Charity triumphed and caused us to forget self preservation and... danger. We were in the midst of the dead and dying who were brought to us by the hundreds... it was necessary to smother our grief and exert ourselves to relieve them."

Before it was all over the French were forced to retreat, covered by Canadien snipers in the woods. Both Wolfe and Montcalm were mortally wounded. Winner and loser, they both died heroes, to be forever remembered.

So, in the end, Wolfe avoided the disgrace he had so feared. On September 18th, 1759, high up on Mountain street in Quebec, the British flag was raised. They had taken the city.

But it wasn't over yet.

Quebec city overlooking the St. Lawrence

XIV
The Battle for North America
Part 1

Quebec was now British—what was left of it. There was confusion and disorder, crumbled walls, ruined crops and a shortage of food, as well as the usual scurvy. Winter was approaching. The small British garrison left behind when the fleet returned to England did their best, along with the Canadiens, to salvage what they could from the mess. But sickness was taking a terrible toll on the British. Since September 18th, 2312 men were ill with scurvy, 682 were dead.

Meanwhile, in Montreal, General de Lévis, Montcalm's replacement, was busy planning to take Quebec back again. Unlike Montcalm, he had no objection to guerilla tactics, and the French troops fought alongside the Canadiens, making a nuisance of themselves around the outskirts of the city, and making it unsafe for the English to venture outside the gates. It was a very long winter.

In the meantime both sides were cut off from Europe, and both were hoping for reinforcements when spring thaw came. At the end of April, 1760, they took up battle positions on the Plains of Abraham, this time with General Murray, the British commander, where Montcalm had been, and Lévis facing them from the other direction, where Wolfe had been. The same mistakes were made. This time it was the English whose soldiers and cannon sank in the spring mud, leaving the French with some advantage. After an indecisive battle of several hours, the French flag flew over the Plains; the Union Jack still flew over Quebec.

Now the two sides waited in suspense to see whose navy would turn up first and save them. After eleven days a ship appeared, sailing up the

St. Lawrence without colours. Only when it reached the walls of Quebec did it put up a flag. The British had won the race. The British Prime Minister, William Pitt, had sent 22 ships with troops, the French only five.

After that Lévis retreated to Montreal, and soon the armies of General Amherst took the city, without battle or fuss. The French capitulated.

The governor, Vaudreuil, did manage to negotiate some very important terms with the British. When the Articles of Capitulation were drawn up, they included a clause about religious freedom: "The free exercise of the Catholic, Apostolic and Roman Religion, shall subsist entire, in such manner that all the states and the people of the towns and countries, places and distant posts, shall continue to assemble in the churches, and to frequent the sacraments as heretofore, without being molested in any manner, directly or indirectly." This was an astonishing concession by the British, considering that Protestant England at the time allowed no religious rights to English Catholics at home.

On September 8th, 1760, half the continent of North America changed hands and became British. George II, king of England, now had 65000 French-speaking Catholic subjects. In 1761 peace talks began in Europe. Some British business men wanted to keep the island of Guadeloupe in the West Indies, and give Canada back to the French, because they made twice as much money from sugar as from furs.

In the end it was agreed that the French would give Canada to the English and receive in return the islands of St. Pierre and Miquelon, and fishing rights in the Gulf of St. Lawrence. This treaty was formalized in 1763, and was known as the treaty of Paris.

XV
The Battle for North America
Part 2

The treaty between England and France had been signed, but not everything had been resolved, not yet. There were still the Natives.

The defeat of the French had spoiled 150 years of native alliances. Pontiac, war chief of the Ottawa, was a firm ally of the French, which says a lot about the French style of diplomacy. The British stopped the exchange of presents, thus showing contempt for the natives and their customs and traditions, and enraging Pontiac. Now there was a new uncertainty. One Ojibwa chief from the west had this to say to some English traders: "Englishmen, although you have conquered the French, you have not conquered us!"

He went on to say that "our Father, the king of France, employed our young men to make war upon your nation," and pointed out that the King of England had not "entered into any treaty with us, therefore he and we are still at war."

The thing the natives feared most were English settlers who, unlike the French traders, cleared and cultivated land and brought a new way of life. Pontiac, war chief of the Ottawa, made plans to capture the forts in the interior, now held by the British. They attacked several forts. At Fort Detroit they killed all the settlers they could find outside its walls, then took prisoners. There followed gruesome scenes of torture and death. The siege went on for months.

In time this native uprising ran out of steam. Some warriors lost interest or went home for the hunting season; smallpox again caused devastation. Sad to say, this time the disease may have been planted on purpose. General

Amherst used an eerily modern method to get rid of the native menace once and for all, (although there is no clear evidence that he succeeded). Small, cut up pieces of an infected blanket were put in small tin boxes and sent back with a delegation from the Ottawa tribe, to be opened when they arrived home at their village. This was an early version of biological warfare.

In 1766 Pontiac signed a peace treaty with the English. Three years later he was assassinated by a native who was angry at being made to give in to the enemy.

The British government, having won this vast, unregulated and barely explored territory, where settlers were already moving westward, did the practical and sensible thing. A royal proclamation was issued in 1763 declaring the interior of the continent to be native land, at least until the British government had made treaties with the native groups of the Ohio Valley.

"We do hereby strictly forbid, on Pain of our Displeasure, all our loving subjects from making any Purchases or Settlements whatever, or taking any possession of any of the lands above reserved, without our especial leave and License".

After this there was peace, for a time.

The man appointed to be governor of this territory was General James Murray. He liked the 65,000 French Catholics under his supervision, but was less keen on the few English-speaking Protestant merchants. One of these, Thomas Walker, wanted an elected legislative assembly which, like in England, would not allow Catholics to vote. Nor did he want French Catholics to sit on juries. Murray saw this as ridiculous, as it would mean that a mere two hundred Protestants would have control of the lives and property of tens of thousands of French subjects, and of the military as well.

This fight over religion and constitutional rights turned first into a court case involving the loud and spiteful Walker, then into violence between the merchants and the military. In the end, even the local British people began to find Walker tiresome.

Walker carried his argument for English-only assembly and juries back to England. But London disagreed with him and agreed with Murray. All Quebec citizens could now sit on juries, and instead of an English-only assembly, there would be no assembly at all.

Eventually Murray was replaced by Guy Carleton, who was of much the same mind as his predecessor. He argued that it was barbaric nonsense to impose English law on a French colony, and in order for things to work smoothly, Quebec had to be accepted as a French colony. In 1770 he returned to London to put before the British parliament his ideas of what Canada should be.

Four years later, in 1774, Carleton's vision was made law. The Quebec Act guaranteed Canadiens the right to their religion, the right to hold public office, and the restoration of French civil law and the seigneurial system of land ownership. Instead of the treatment that a conquered people might expect, they were granted a colony and a way of life which were hardly different from what they had known before the beginning of the Seven Years War.

XVI
The American Revolution

The American colonies were not happy. They felt betrayed by the Quebec Act which left one million American colonists hemmed in by a mere 65 thousand French; they imagined themselves slaves to Catholics and French civil law, and felt their own law was endangered. On top of that they felt frustrated because they were being prevented from moving into the Ohio Valley.

Already they were good and angry about being taxed to help pay off Britain's war debts, but now, they thought, this was the last straw. Soon there were riots in Massachusetts. A screaming mob charged at some hapless British soldiers who had been sent to keep order; the soldiers fired back. Paul Revere engraved, printed and distributed an exaggerated, inflammatory and somewhat fanciful account of the incident, and before you could say "tabloid", the event became known as the "Boston Massacre". The people were already inflamed with a sense of grievance, and this was like pouring on gasoline. It wasn't long before added grievances turned into rebellion, and in 1775 the American Revolution began.

Not all Americans in the Thirteen Colonies were against the British government, however; and not all the British in the new Canada were for it. In Quebec the permanently disgruntled Thomas Walker was busy stirring up trouble. Each side tried to gain support from the other. The French for the most part tried to stay out of the quarrel, regarding it as just a civil war between two sorts of Englishmen; moreover, they were afraid of the Americans. As things became heated, Canadien militias were called up, martial law was declared. In the American colonies rebellion was shouted, statues were defaced, scary rumours were spread about, insults and slurs flew back and forth, tempers ran high, and the word "republic" was heard more and more often.

George Washington, then commander of American forces, saw the French presence as a threat; he wanted all of Canada to belong to America. In 1775 American troops invaded Quebec.

Both sides spent a miserable autumn and winter. At first Montreal capitulated; the city of Quebec was besieged for the fourth time in its short history; confusion reigned. Sir Guy Carleton, the governor of Quebec, at least had a strong ally in the Catholic church, which announced that anyone who took up arms against the King would be excommunicated.

The American who led the assault on Quebec City was Major-General Benedict Arnold, (later joined from Montreal by Brigadier-General Richard Montgomery). Arnold began the campaign bravely enough, but there were too many difficulties to overcome. Eventually the army was defeated by inadequate maps, bad weather, starvation, smallpox and pneumonia and, as always, the onset of winter. In Montreal the occupying troops lost whatever goodwill the inhabitants might have shown them because of bad manners, looting, vandalism, and generally rotten behaviour, much to the shame and embarrassment of their commanding officers. By December 31st most of the soldiers' enlistment contracts had expired, and many of them, unwilling as they had been in the first place, took the opportunity to disappear and go home, where they concentrated on tormenting their royalist neighbours.

By now the American colonies were deeply and cruelly divided—Republicans against Tories—with farm against farm, town against town, even family members one against another. Americans suspected by Republicans of being royalist and sympathizing with the British government were put in prison, beaten, lynched, tarred and feathered, their property taken away, their houses burned. Law was forgotten, chaos ruled. Huge numbers of these royalists were forced to leave the country. Some went back to England, some to the West Indies. There were long wagon trains, mostly of women and children, heading north to Canada—at first to Quebec refugee camps.

Some of these Loyalists, as they were called, were native Indians of the Six Nations. Their allegiance to the British left the Americans with practically no native allies. Joseph Brant was a Mohawk chief who fought for the British. He believed that if the Americans became independent of Britain the Mohawks would lose their land. He was a clever, English-educated man, at home in both European and native cultures; his Mohawk name, oddly enough, meant "He Who Places Two Bets". Brant assembled a native fighting force from four of the Six Nations: the Mohawk, Cayuga, Onondaga and Seneca. Together with John Butler, a rich land owner from the Mohawk Valley, and his Rangers, they caused havoc and terror among the American rebels on the frontier.

George Washington decided to retaliate. Within just two months he had achieved his objective—the nearly complete destruction of the Six Nations' towns and settlements, forty in all, in the Mohawk Valley.

In 1783 the (second) Treaty of Paris was signed, in which Britain recognised American independence, (which had already been declared by the Americans seven years before). But in the treaty there was no mention of the Six Nations or their part in the struggle. The natives were naturally shocked and insulted at being thus forgotten.

Brant went to London for a meeting with King George III to seek compensation for the Mohawk land lost in the war. He was cordially received, even granted money to build a church. But he would not kneel before the king. "I bow to no man" he said, "for I am considered a prince among my own people. But I will gladly shake your hand".

To make up for the lost land the British government granted compensation in the form of 275,000 hectares of land in the British territory north of Lake Erie, where Brant and his followers settled. There he lived like an Englishman in a beautiful large house with slaves and servants, built the first Anglican church in Upper Canada, and translated parts of the Bible into Mohawk.

As for John Butler and his Rangers, they were given land on the west bank of the Niagara River. The daughter of one of these men wrote: "My father settled on his land near the fort. He drew an axe and a hoe from the government.........My mother had a cow, a bed, six plates and three knives......Men, women and children all went to work clearing the land. There were none to make improvements in [Upper] Canada then but the United Empire Loyalists, and they planted the germ of its future greatness".

XVII
The War of 1812
Part 1

Since 1776 the continent was no longer just British North America; now two distinct countries were emerging: British Canada and independent-minded America, each with its own worries, ambitions and views. The Loyalists, those who chose Canada, wanted more than just land; they wanted their own colony. The English loyalists of course wanted English law. The French "Canadiens" wanted their own French elected assembly.

The solution was to create two distinct provinces, which were made by separating the province of Quebec into two districts. Each had its own culture, law and land tenure, and its own elected assembly. In 1791 King George III signed a bill dividing Quebec into Upper and Lower Canada.

The first Lieutenant-Governor was John Graves Simcoe. He came from England to find a wilderness area the size of France with only 10,000 people in it. At first he and his wife lived in what is now Niagara-on-the-Lake, in a tent. He wanted to recreate a little Britain, and he went to work with a right good will, even going so far as to sing "God Save the King" every night before bed. He thought this Britishness might lure some of the Americans who were finding that their new democracy, now that Britain had been thrust aside, had lost some of its lustre. He advertised in English and West Indian newspapers, offering them land: for an oath of loyalty to the Crown and a promise to till the soil there would be a reward of 200 acres for every white immigrant. Also, since the elections of 1792 all male property owners could vote. People came from afar to take the offer. By 1812 the new immigrants outnumbered the original Loyalists four to one.

Meanwhile, Napoleon and his armies were busy battling their way across Europe, causing misery and destruction from Madrid to Moscow in an attempt to take over the continent in the name of revolutionary France. England was trying to stop them.

The War of 1812 was an extension of this struggle. In Lower Canada the elected assembly was mostly French, (although the legislative and executive branches were controlled by English appointees). James Craig, the new governor, was afraid the "Canadiens" would side with Napoleon. There were rumours of invasion by the French fleet; people were afraid the Americans would join the French against the English; there was fear of the Americans invading Canada. (In fact, some "Canadiens" were among Britain's staunchest supporters, preferring English liberty, constitution and parliamentary democracy to French ways).

In Upper Canada the Brigadier general of British forces was Sir Isaac Brock. He knew the Americans were hostile—the newspapers were full of it. One American congressman stated that, as the St. Lawrence and Mississippi rivers interlocked in several places, it was God's will that Britain's territories should belong to the United States.

On June 18, 1812, President James Madison of the United States declared war on Canada. Many Americans thought it would be a walk-over. After all, the American population now out-numbered Canada's 14 to 1. Brock had a 2,000 kilometre border to defend with only 1600 troops, not all of them reliable. The situation looked hopeless; defence seemed impossible.

So Brock chose to attack. Fort Detroit was defended by 2000 men and was a week's march away. Brock had only 300 British troops and 400 Canadian militia. But he also had 600 natives led by Tecumseh.

Tecumseh was a handsome, charming Shawnee chief who had spent much of his life trying to prevent Americans from taking native lands in the Ohio Valley. He was also, apparently, fond of Shakespearean theatre. Certainly his tactics for taking Detroit had a theatrical flavour. First he paraded his 600 warriors—in full war paint of bright red, some caked in blue clay, some tattooed from head to foot—in front of Fort Detroit. Then he did it two more times for good measure. This made it look as if there were thousands of them. Brock had scrounged some old cast-off British uniforms for his Canadian militia, to make them look more professional.

The whole force assembled in view of Fort Detroit. Then Brock sent a letter to the American commander, General Hull, warning him that once battle commenced he, Brock, would not be able to control the Indian troops. Hull had civilians in the fort, including some of his own family. The horror induced by the very thought of "Indian massacre" was enough. Fort Detroit surrendered. Brock acquired 2000 prisoners, all their muskets and cannon, and enough money to pay his troops. All this by bluffing, and without anyone getting killed.

Of course the Americans felt humiliated, and immediately tried to regain their honour by attacking Queenston Heights, firing their artillery from across the Niagara River. Their chances were not good, even at the start. Their leader, Major Lovett, was a poet and pacifist; their troops' loyalty was uncertain and there were many desertions—the militia was not required to fight on foreign soil. When the Americans tried to cross the river they ran into trouble; there were no boats large enough to carry the big guns, and the current was almost too strong for the smaller boats. They did manage to land, and found a steep path up the cliff. By guts and determination, and even threats to their own troops, they actually captured Queenston Heights. Brock then tried to take back the high ground. Alas, his scarlet tunic was an easy target and he was shot and killed instantly.

Finally the natives came to the Canadian defence, led by a son of Joseph Brant, and by one of his adopted nephews, Major John Norton, half Scottish and half Cherokee. When British reinforcements arrived, together they charged the Americans, who by now had been driven to the mountain's edge and had nowhere left to go. Many of them leaped off the cliff, rather than face capture by the Indians, and were dashed to pieces on the rocks below. Those Americans who had crossed the river but were still at the bottom of the cliff were unable to move. For some time they tried to surrender, until at last they were heard, fortunately before there was a complete slaughter. Nine hundred and twenty-five Americans surrendered and there were two hundred and fifty casualties. Of the Canadians only fourteen were dead and seventy-seven wounded. Unfortunately that included Major General Sir Isaac Brock.

XVIII
The War of 1812
Part 2

More than anyone else, William Henry Harrison, Governor of Indiana Territory, was the person responsible for the American Indians losing their land. He was not a nice man, it seems. By deceit, fraud, bullying and whiskey he had managed to buy up more than 40 million hectares—that is to say, half of present-day Indiana plus parts of Wisconsin, Illinois and Missouri. He wanted to fill them with settlers and build himself an empire in the American Midwest.

He was also afraid of Tecumseh. This man, he thought, was charismatic and powerful enough to build his own native empire, rivalling that of Mexico. Obviously the two men were enemies.

When war broke out Tecumseh and his warriors joined a British force against Harrison. But events went against them. Through a series of mistakes and failures Tecumseh and his men were finally left to fight alone—500 of them against 3,000 Americans in a fierce hand-to-hand battle at Moraviantown on the Detroit River. A British soldier later met some natives in the woods who told him that they had beaten back the American, but that their leader, Tecumseh, was dead.

No one to this day knows what became of Tecumseh's body. Dozens of men *claimed* to have killed him. The death of Tecumseh meant the end of his dream of a Native Indian state, and it influenced American politics for a long time. William Henry Harrison even became President for a short while; and for half a century afterward American children could be heard chanting the rhyme: "Rumpsey, Dumpsey, who killed Tecumseh?"

After this success against the British, Harrison was poised to take Upper Canada. But his army was now out of supplies and besides, the British were saved for the time being by their old ally Winter. Harrison retreated to Detroit.

In a second attempt, meanwhile, on Lower Canada, the British and Canadiens braved foul autumn weather, out-lasting the Americans in the cold and rain. The Americans finally gave up on Lower Canada and started to look westward, also toward Upper Canada. More and bloodier fighting continued, with more shifting back and forth of loyalties and sides, some men being hanged for treason, and many settlements burned, including most of the Niagara Peninsula.

The bloodiest of all was the Battle of Lundy's Lane, in July of 1814 near Willson's tavern, a pub overlooking Niagara Falls. The fighting took place in a graveyard near Lundy's farm, where the British had been waiting in the dark. The two sides were so close that they could see each other's faces in a ghastly blue smokey flash every time a gun was discharged. For hours they fought hand-to-hand, desperate and half blind, sometimes killing their own men by mistake. At midnight the fighting stopped without a word being said, and the Americans retreated. Nearly 2000 dead were left on the field.

In August, 1814, the British marched on Washington and burned most of it, including the White House and the Library of Congress.

On Christmas Eve, 1814, the Treaty of Ghent marked the official end of the war. Britain agreed to return all the territories she had seized, and at last acknowledged that her American colonies were lost forever. From now on North America south of the Great Lakes would be the United States of America, and to the north—Canada.

XIX
Voyageurs

So far you've heard the 800-year-long story of how North America was discovered by Europeans and eventually divided into the United States and Canada. But that was happening in the eastern part of the continent. What about the West? To find that out we must go back a few hundred years, to the beginnings of the fur trade.

You may remember that (after Cartier) Champlain was the first European to become aware of the vast river network that acts as a water-highway system leading to the interior of the continent. He was also the first to understand the importance of the canoe in travelling this land of deep forest, rock and churning water, where European modes of transport wouldn't have a hope, and where travel was only possible by water. He knew that whoever controlled those water routes controlled the trade of half a continent.

The history of exploration in North America, covering more territory than ever, anywhere, before or since, is just as dramatic and exciting as any in the history of the world. Europeans hundreds of years ago thought of North America as the Dark Continent, just like Australia or rainforest Africa in later centuries. Yet, by the mid 1700s French explorers and their Native partners in the fur trade had already gone all the way down the Mississippi and as far west as the Rockies—this at a time when the Americans, with more than twenty times the Canadien population, were just starting to venture over the Appalachians.

None of this would have been possible without the Natives, the Métis and the canoe. Without them there would have been no Canada. Today we remember the names of famous explorers and mapmakers, from the days of New France to the Geological Survey of Canada in the late 1800s - after all, many lakes and rivers are named after them. But the people who helped them along, carrying their packs and paddling their canoes, (and sometimes piggy-backing them ashore so their feet didn't get wet), were the voyageurs.

Nowadays we think of the voyageur as a colourful character wearing a sash around his waist, a toque or kerchief on his head, and singing his jaunty songs to the rhythm of the paddle. What we don't think about is how hard a life he led. He would paddle hard, 50 strokes a minute, 30,000 strokes a day, often upstream, with frequent portages, through clouds of mosquitoes and blackflies, and with a pretty monotonous diet to look forward to at the end of the day. On top of that would be the dangers of heart-stopping rapids and sharp rocks lurking beneath the water waiting to rip open the canoe. This went on week after week, year after year, until by the time he was thirty his health would probably be shot.

What Father Pierre-François-Xavier Charlevoix wrote in the 1740s could just as well be talking about the voyageurs of the Geological Survey at the turn of the 20th century: "The journeys they undertake; the fatigues they undergo; the dangers to which they expose themselves; and the efforts they make surpass all imagination".

"Voyageurs at Dawn", painting by Frances Anne Hopkins, 1871

Beginning letter of the HBC Charter, with a picture of Charles II

XX
Radishes and Gooseberries and the HBC

Far away to the north another group of fur traders were to become instrumental in pushing exploration and, eventually, in settling the West. This is the strange story of the Hudson Bay Company, which owes its very existence to an aging Englishman, two Frenchmen, and a fashion in men's hats.

After the death of Queen Elizabeth, and following the great Elizabethans like Drake, Frobisher and others, all seeking the North-West Passage, along came Henry Hudson. In 1610 the East India Company and the North-West Passage Company put up the money for another try. Hudson was a good navigator, courageous and imaginative, but he was already getting too old for this, and he was not the best leader of men.

In his ship, the Discovery, Hudson braved treacherous tides and ice along what we know as Hudson Strait, then entered (the future) Hudson Bay, thinking it was the Pacific. But after wandering around what we now know as James Bay, it became clear that this was not the way to China. His crew, who had been promised bonuses if they succeeded, were more than just disappointed. When the Discovery set sail for home after a miserable winter, the men mutinied. Hudson and seven men, including his son, were put in a small boat and set adrift. The Discovery sailed away and left them to die.

Strangely, much good came from this voyage. The mutineers from Hudson's ship took back with them knowledge of the route to the west and of the old native trading networks in the areas Hudson had explored. About the same time, beaver hats became all the rage in Europe—so much so, in fact, that the Indians thought the Europeans were silly. One Indian friend of Father Le Jeune, the Jesuit superior in Quebec in the 1630s, said to him one day when showing him a very beautiful knife, "The English have no sense; they give us twenty knives like this for one beaver skin". Later the King of England would issue a charter to start a new fur trading venture which would lead, in time, to the opening of the Canadian West. The charter was born of an Englishman's geographic knowledge; but the idea for the company itself was the brainchild of two Frenchmen: Pierre Esprit Radisson and Médart Couart Groseilliers, known to generations of English-speaking school children as "Radishes and Gooseberries".

Pierre Radisson was from Provence, but came to New France as a teenager. From the start he felt himself to be a man of destiny, a discoverer of "wild nations"; this we know from his journals. Soon after his arrival in 1651 in New France he was kidnapped by the Iroquois during a raid and adopted by a prominent native family. He lived the native life, learned the language, hunted and went on war parties with them. Once he tried to escape to return to Trois Rivìeres. He was caught, tortured, and would have died but for his adoptive family. When they all visited Fort Orange (now Albany in New York State), the governor offered a ransom for Radisson; but Radisson said politely no thank you and returned with the Iroquois. Perhaps this was a ruse to put them off guard because, not long after that, he again tried to escape, this time with success.

Groseilliers was Radisson's brother-in-law and a fur trader who already knew the country as far west as Lake Huron. In 1659 they decided to team up to explore past the territory already known to Europeans and find new sources of fur. They proposed this to the governor but he, being what today might be called a control freak, insisted they take government officials with them, as well as giving back half their profits. When the two explorers objected the governor became annoyed and commanded them not to go without his permission.

This was too much. In the middle of the night they left, paddled away and kept on paddling for two months: up the Ottawa River, through Lake Nipissing, to the north shore of Lake Huron. On the way they met Iroquois who were jealously guarding the route to the interior. A nasty battle ensued but, aided by some Ojibwa, they overcame their attackers and continued on. By winter they had reached Lake Superior and made camp with a group of Ojibwa. This was the farthest west any European had been.

That winter they nearly starved to death. When food ran out they had to eat their dogs, then tree bark, then the hide from beaver pelts. Some of the Ojibwa did die of starvation, and those who were left looked like skeletons.

The survivors were rewarded when, in the spring, the Ojibwa attended the Feast of the Dead, and Radisson and Groseilliers went with them. Eighteen native tribes came together for ten days of feasting, dancing, singing and politicking near Lake Superior. It was a great trading opportunity. Gifts were exchanged back and forth, and Radisson and Groseilliers were given more than 300 beaver robes. They were also told that there were even thicker, more beautiful pelts to be found at a "great northern bay".

Radisson and Groseilliers returned in triumph to Montreal, along with 300 natives in canoes laden with furs. But instead of being welcomed with applause and thanks, they were fined by the governor and Groseilliers was even thrown in jail for a time. They had planned to look for those wonderful furs on their next trip, but after such a reception in Montreal, (and an equally disappointing one later in Paris), they decided to take their business elsewhere.

In 1665 they went to England. The British East India Company had just been chartered and there was much interest in North American commercial possibilities. King Charles II received them and agreed to finance a voyage to Hudson Bay to seek out those furs. In 1668 they set out for Hudson Bay, Radisson on the "Eaglet" and Groseilliers on the "Nonsuch". A storm at sea caused Radisson to turn back, but Groseilliers went on. He returned a year later with a large cargo of beautiful beaver pelts and the knowledge of the best way to get them. In 1670 Charles II issued a charter granting monopoly trading privileges and mineral rights to all the lands with waters draining into Hudson Bay and James Bay. This territory was fifteen times the size of Britain, and in honour of Prince Rupert, the king's cousin, it was named Rupert's Land.

Thus was born the Hudson Bay Company (HBC).

Hudson Bay Co. ships, 1769

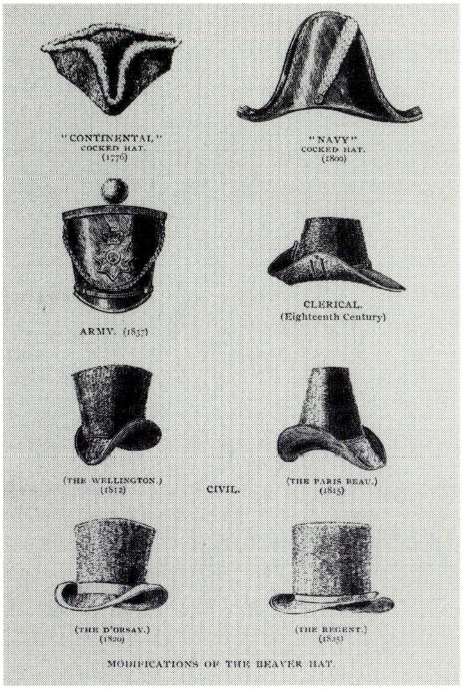

An engraving of different styles of beaver hat

XXI
La Vérendrye and Henday

The company that Radisson and Groseilliers helped create flourished. The Cree had traded amongst themselves for a long time; now they had a new trading partner in the HBC. There was also a new trade rivalry between the French and the English, and the Cree turned it to their advantage.

The Hudson Bay Company system at first depended on the natives bringing furs all the way to the posts on Hudson Bay and James Bay, sometimes over hundreds of miles. Once a year there would be a big trading session. This began with the passing of a ceremonial pipe which the Cree left at the fort to show they would be back the next year. Then came the exchange of gifts and the speeches, and then the real business. A Cree chief said to the traders: "You told me last year to bring many Indians. You see I have not lied. Here is a great many young men ....We have come a long way to see you. The French send for us but we will not be there. We love the English....Do you understand me?" The natives were tough business men and insisted on the very best in trade goods like guns, knives and tobacco. The Europeans did their best to please them.

Meanwhile, at a French trading post near Lake Superior, a trader named Pierre Gaultier de Varennes, Sieur de la Vérendrye, was listening very carefully to the natives. They told of a river route that led to the Western Sea. La Vérendrye was sure it would lead to China. To get the governor's interest he proposed a route that would cut across the trapping grounds of the natives who traded with the HBC. He was sure those natives would be happy to bring their furs to the French instead, if given the chance. He was right. But the Cree wanted to test his friendship by demanding that he send his son Jean-Baptiste with them in a war party. Jean-Baptiste went, and was later killed by the Sioux in a revenge raid.

By 1743 La Vérendrye had established eight trading posts and staked out a huge new territory for New France that extended to the foothills of the Rocky Mountains. He had laid the foundations for a fur trading empire that rivalled the HBC.

The Hudson Bay Company's answer to La Vérendrye was Anthony Henday. Henday was a labourer who volunteered to travel inland to the natives to seek out new sources of fur. In June of 1754 Henday left to paddle down the Hayes River. Then he walked with a group of natives to what is today Red Deer, Alberta. He was the first Englishman to meet the Blackfoot, and one of the first to see the great buffalo herds moving across the prairie, darkening the land as far as the eye could see, the earth seeming to heave as if from an earthquake.

Henday spent the winter with the Blackfoot and hunted with them. The Blackfoot were charming hosts, but were not interested in trading with the English—it was too far to Hudson Bay and they did not paddle. They were proud horsemen of the plains, and besides, the French were already coming to them. After a year Henday went home to Hudson Bay, with only a few inferior furs and the bad news.

Then, almost overnight, things changed. It was 1759, in the middle of the Seven Years War, and the northern half of North America was no longer French, but British. Now Scottish merchants from Quebec came west to trade, using the old trading network established by the French. The natives did not take kindly to the new people, at first. These independent Scotsmen and adventurers from the Thirteen Colonies began spending winters living with the natives to gain their trust, and before long they were taking profits away from the HBC. The "pedlars", as they were called, were finding rich new territories, while the HBC depended on the well known territory near Hudson Bay. Soon the new traders eliminated even the competition amongst themselves—they formed a company.

In 1774, more than a hundred years after the Hudson Bay charter, the North West Company was born.

XXII
Samuel Hearne

The Hudson Bay Company was run by business men, far away on the other side of the Atlantic Ocean. The new North West Company was run by men with hands-on experience in the fur trade. These Nor'westers took their trade to the natives, made friends with them and often married native wives, making the business a family affair. Following La Vérendrye's routes they went as far north as Lake Athabaska and west to the Peace River country. So it was not surprising that they were soon bringing in four times as many furs as the HBC, and getting very rich. Clearly, the HBC would have to do something.

They had begun by sending men from Hudson Bay posts to the natives, to get them to bring their furs to York Factory. Now they would have to do more than that. They would have to establish posts in the interior and bring trade to the natives, the way the Nor'westers did.

One of the first HBC expeditions to the interior was not to find furs, but minerals. To this end they sent a Dene native named Matonabbee to follow the largest rivers to the north. Matonabbee returned with a map of the Coppermine River drawn in charcoal on a deerskin. Two years later the difficult task of retracing Matonabbee's route into this harsh, unknown land, and returning with copper, was given to Samuel Hearne.

Hearne was chosen for the job because he was young, tough, a fighter and navigator, and he knew how to snowshoe. He made two unsuccessful attempts before the third and final expedition, which we know about from his famous journal published as "A Journey from Prince of Wales Fort in Hudson Bay to the Northern Ocean". Apparently Matonabbee blamed the first two failed attempts on bad guides and the absence of women. Said he: "When all the men are heavy laden they can neither hunt nor travel to any considerable distance. Women were made for labour. One of them can carry, or haul, as much as two men can do. They also pitch our tents, make and mend our clothing....in fact there is no such thing as travelling any distance without their assistance". On this third trip Matonabbee brought women, including his many wives.

They set off from Churchill in the winter of 1770. Hearne describes Matonabbee as being tall, handsome and brave: "I have met with few Christians who possessed more good moral qualities or fewer bad ones." He was also a fierce warrior, a clever diplomat and an experienced guide, all of which Hearne needed, especially when faced with other natives trying to rob them. Eventually they reached the land of the Copper Indian, who clustered around Hearne like zoologists around a rare animal. They had never before seen a European. After examining him from head to foot they proclaimed him to be a perfect specimen. They thought him almost beautiful, except for his colouring which they considered unpleasantly pale.

By the time they reached the tundra they had run out of food and were getting too weak to carry their packs—Hearne's pack contained the sextant which weighed sixty pounds. Worse still, they ran into some Dene natives who were spoiling for a fight with their old enemies, the "Eskimaux". Hearne tried to talk them out of it, but the Dene went ahead and painted their faces red and black, tied their hair back, and stripped down to their breechcloths. Then, at one in the morning, they attacked their victims while they slept. Hearne watched, helpless and stricken with horror, as more than twenty Inuit were slaughtered. For the rest of his life he could hardly think of that day without weeping. He named the place where it happened Bloody Fall.

They had reached the Coppermine River, but in spite of much digging and searching they only found one nugget of any decent size. So they turned around and walked home—a journey of 4,000 kilometres.

Hearne's expedition was not a commercial success. But he was the first European to reach the arctic overland, a huge step forward in opening up the interior. He went on to establish Cumberland House, the HBC's first inland trading post. Later he became the factor at Fort Prince of Wales, where he delighted in making pets of some of the animals around, like muskrats, geese, foxes and beaver. As he wrote in his journal, "They become so domesticated as to answer their name, and follow...as a dog would do... and were much pleased at being fondled. During the winter they lived on the same food as the women and were remarkably fond of rice and plum pudding."

Bloody Fall

XXIII
The West Coast

About the same time that the fur trade was moving from the East, across the continent toward the Rockies, the British were coming from the other direction and having a look at the West Coast. Until the late 1800s the West beyond the Rocky Mountains was quite isolated and separate from the rest of the Northwest, and even more mysterious to Europeans.

Strangely enough, the earliest written reference to the Pacific Northwest is by, not a European, but a Buddhist monk named Hwui Shan, who travelled across the "Great Eastern Sea" from China in 458 AD. He stopped first at the Aleutian Islands and later on the mainland, and described the natives as having strange markings on their foreheads. He said they were merry, good-natured and hospitable.

Then there is evidence that another Chinese expedition visited the Pacific Northwest in the early 1400s, this time in large ships meant for serious exploration. These expeditions were later stopped, and in time forgotten, when the rulers of China decided to shut out the world instead of exploring it. But there are still West Coast native stories about foreign visitors from long ago, whom they called "Eaters of Maggots". Otherwise there was little contact with visitors from another continent. The Spanish (and later, Americans) came up the coast to trade during the two or three hundred years after Columbus' landing in the New World, and Drake on his circling of the globe sailed up past the Pacific Northwest coast. But the first European to come and stay any length of time was Captain Cook.

James Cook, the son of a Scottish farmer, was the greatest navigator, explorer and geographer of his time. He sailed around the world twice, commanded a ship during the Seven Years War, and mapped the coast of Newfoundland. He is perhaps best known for his voyages through the

South Pacific in the mid-to-late 18th century. He was also the first to find a cure for scurvy, which had been killing ships' crews for as long as there had been long sea voyages. He experimented with citrus fruits, sauerkraut and other foods, and did not lose a single man to scurvy on his Pacific voyages.

On a third such voyage in the 1770s he set off to look for a North-West Passage. He sailed east across the Pacific and in 1778 landed in Nootka Sound on Vancouver Island, where his men began trading with the Nootka (Nuu-chah-nulth) for otter pelts. On this trip his crew included George Vancouver and William Bligh, (who later became the notorious captain of "Mutiny on the Bounty"). Cook describes the natives in his journal: "Sometimes they wear carved wooden masks... applied on the face or to the forehead. Some of these resemble human faces, furnished with hair, beards and eyebrows; others the heads of birds...and many the heads of land and sea animals...The houses are disposed in three ranges or rows...The height of the sides of these habitations is seven or eight feet....The planks that compose the roof slant forward; they are laid on loose and are moved to let out smoke and admit air or light....Many are decorated with images. These are nothing more than the trunks of very large trees...with the front carved into a human face, the arms and hands cut out upon the sides, and variously painted, so that the whole is a truly monstrous figure...The women were always properly clothed, and behaved with the utmost propriety... and modesty."

Cook noticed the same markings on native foreheads as those that Hwui Shan had recorded in his journal more than 1300 years before. He also took note of the complex system of native trading networks, political structures, laws and customs, and their many different language groups. He knew that his exploration would eventually lead to European settlement, and he was worried about the effect this would have on the natives.

After his historic stay on the West Coast, Cook sailed on into the Bering Strait in search of the Passage (west to east), but was discouraged by a wall of ice. Later, stopping at the Sandwich Islands (Hawaii) he was killed by natives on Kealakekua Beach, on Valentine's Day, 1779.

Cook was not the first to explore the Northwest coast, but he and his men were the first to make it interesting to Europeans, and set the stage for what was to come.

Captain Cook

Two West Coast chiefs

XXIV
Alexander Mackenzie

Toward the end of the 18th century people in Europe were getting quite excited about the West, thanks to new maps and explorers' journals, and particularly the published accounts of Captain Cook. But still no one had found that Passage to the western sea. The Hudson Bay Company was working on it, so in 1789 the North West Company decided to commission someone to do the same.

Alexander Mackenzie was the man. At the age of twenty-five he was given the task of finding a route to the Pacific, then sailing up the coast to Alaska, across to Russia, and back to England. Unlike other explorers such as Hearne, Mackenzie was not much interested in beautiful landscape and native folklore. He was just interested in success, and wanted to get the job done. On his first trip he covered more than 1700 kilometres in only two weeks, from Fort Chipewyan on Lake Athabaska down what is now the Mackenzie River—but to the Arctic Ocean instead of the Pacific. The trip was not a commercial success. He decided to return to England for a winter in order to gather proper equipment and better knowledge of astronomy and navigation.

Mackenzie learned from his mistakes. On his second voyage he had a compass, a sextant, a chronometer, a telescope, and a reasonable knowledge of navigation. In May of 1793, with nine men and a dog, he paddled up the Peace River, looking for the continental divide. He managed to cross the Rockies and in June reached the Fraser River on the other side. Shuswap natives warned him that the river was too dangerous and advised him to use the overland route that they used for trading with other tribes on the coast.

After a month of walking, Mackenzie and his party reached Dean Channel, where they were met by a hostile group of Bella Bella natives. In spite of the threat to him and his terrified men, Mackenzie stopped and set up his instruments to calculate the position of the sun and fix their latitude and longitude—in other words, to determine precisely where on earth they were. He also left his mark on a large rock. He mixed up some vermillion with some grease and wrote in large letters:

ALEXANDER MACKENZIE FROM CANADA, BY LAND.

THE 22nd OF JULY, ONE THOUSAND SEVEN HUNDRED AND NINETY-THREE.

Mackenzie had reached the salt water of the Pacific Ocean. He was the first European to cross the continent over land.

A version of Mackenzie's journal was published, and stirred up a good deal of interest in both Europe and the United States. Napoleon read it, and so did Thomas Jefferson, who immediately commissioned Lewis and Clark to map the territory west of the Mississippi. Mackenzie was knighted by King George III, went home to Scotland and, unlike most explorers, died a rich man.

Alexander Mackenzie

Memorial inscription at Bella Coola, done with bear grease and vermillion; touched up a bit in 1926 and still readable

XXV
David Thompson

This is a story about a lonely, poor little boy and how, through education, ambition, and the kindness of strangers, he rose to become one of the greatest men of his time.

David Thompson was born in 1770 in London, of Welsh parents. He was only seven years old when he became an orphan—he had no parents and no money—so he was taken into the Grey Coat Hospital, a charity school for the poor run by the Church. There he learned to read and write. From the start he loved arithmetic and math problems, and he loved reading—books like "Robinson Crusoe" and "Gulliver's Travels", about solitary travellers and adventurers.

When he was fourteen he joined the Hudson Bay Company as an apprentice, hoping for similar adventures. For the first year he served under Samuel Hearne at Churchill Factory, where he was put to work as a clerk making inventory lists in alphabetical order: flannel, flint, gin, hardtack, hatchets, etc. It was intensely cold in winter, hot and mosquito-infested in summer—decidedly more uncomfortable than adventurous. But even then Thompson's scientific curiosity caused him to overcome discomfort and examine the mosquitoes under a microscope, recording details of their system for sucking blood.

Of all the great explorers Thompson was probably the most practical and scientific-minded, yet he also became a devout Christian. He describes the event that converted him:

"A strange incident happened to me....I was sitting at a small table with the chequer board before me, when the devil sat down opposite to me; his features and colour were those of a Spaniard, he had two short black horns on his forehead which pointed forewards; his head and body down to his waist....was covered with glossy black curling hair....We began playing..... and he lost every game;....at length he got up and disappeared. My eyes were open, it was broad daylight....was it a dream or was it reality? I could not decide."

Thompson remained true to his faith for the rest of his life. He felt that God had given him "the power to examine His works on our globe".

After a year at Churchill Factory Thompson at last got a taste of adventure. He was asked to travel to York Factory with two Cree Indians, to deliver mail. Off he went, equipped with just a blanket and a gun. "Every day," he wrote, "we passed from 12 to 15 polar bears, lying a short distance from the shore....The Indian rule is to walk past them....without seeming to notice them".

The next year, when he was seventeen, Thompson was given the task of building a trading post on the western plains. It was then that he saw the vastness of the interior for the first time: "At length the Rocky Mountains came in sight, like shining white clouds on the horizon. As we proceeded they rose in height, their immense masses of snow appeared above the clouds and formed an impassable barrier, even to the eagle."

He was also amazed by another sight, a huge city of tents where thousands of Peigan natives had set up camp. Thompson spent that winter in the tent of an elder named Saukamapee, who told him stories and taught him the language. One of the stories was very sad:

The Peigan had crept up to the camp of an enemy, intending to attack them; but when they slit open the tents, their "eyes were appalled with terror; there was none to fight but the dead and the dying...." They were dying of smallpox, a disease against which the natives had no immunity. The Peigan made the mistake of seizing the enemies' possessions and taking them home. They had no idea that one person could infect another. Within a day or two, "this dreadful disease broke out in our camp," Saukamapee said, "and spread from one tent to another as if the bad spirit carried it.... We shall never be again the same people".

When Thompson was twenty years old he broke his leg, and was resting at Cumberland House waiting for it to mend, when he met the chief surveyor for the HBC, Philip Turnor. Now he knew what he wanted to do for the rest of his life. After becoming Turnor's assistant, he brushed up his math, learned practical astronomy, and studied all day and long into the night. He worked with such dedication, with only one candle, that he strained his eyes and lost the sight of one eye.

By the end of his apprenticeship, Thompson was half blind but still determined to be a surveyor. Normally when an employee had finished his apprenticeship the HBC gave him a suit of clothes. Thompson wrote to headquarters in London asking if he might have a set of surveying instruments instead. The HBC sent him both.

For the next twenty years Thompson measured the latitude and longitude of everywhere he went on his ceaseless travels. The natives teased him fondly and called him "Man Who Looks at Stars". He tried to explain that he looked at the heavens in order to measure the distance and direction from one place to another. They shook their heads in disbelief and said why didn't he just look at the ground, not the stars.

Thompson's reputation was growing and spreading, and soon the North West Company lured him away from the HBC, offering him more scope to do his chosen work. Competition was fierce now as there was not enough beaver to go around. Both companies were anxious to push their territories north and west, and to find a route to the Pacific that was easier and more practical than the one Mackenzie had found.

In 1799 Thompson married a Métis woman named Charlotte Small. He was 29 years old, she was 13. From then on he took her and his growing family with him on long trips, when he wandered the great plains taking instrument readings from the stars and making notes. In a span of 25 years he walked or paddled more than 5,000 miles (8,000 kilometres), living sometimes for years at a time in a tent. He surveyed more territory than anyone else before him. His 77 journals included descriptions of the territory west of Lake Superior; the 49th parallel, which became part of the boundary between Canada and the United States; details about rivers, native customs, beliefs and languages; the habits of moose, deer, fox, field mice. He made not just maps, but pictures of a whole new world that Europeans could understand.

The North West Company still wanted Thompson to find a convenient route to the Pacific, to establish trade with the west coast natives and, eventually, with China. Thompson had by this time been living for nearly two years in a tent, and had hoped to return to civilization. But he pressed on into the Rocky Mountain foothills, the home of his old friends the Peigan. Unfortunately in the meantime the North West Company had been selling guns to the Flatheads, the traditional enemies of the Peigan. In a rage, the Peigan chased Thompson through the forest along the foothills, then blocked his way into the mountains. There was nothing else for it—Thompson would have to go the long way round.

For two months they travelled a detour through an avalanche zone. In some places the snow was almost as high as a house. The horses they had with them were no use and had to be left behind. Soon most of his men deserted as well. Nevertheless, every night Thompson set up his instruments and his little portable desk and spent an hour or so fixing and mapping their position. He was entranced by this wilderness, by the brilliance of the night sky full of stars, and felt he could almost reach out and touch them. He felt very close to God.

In this manner Thompson at last crossed the mountains and made camp, where he waited for winter to end. In the spring he made a canoe, (from cedar instead of birch bark), and became the first European to explore the Columbia River. He met the Simpoil, Nespelim, Methow and Wenatchee natives and convinced them to trade with the North West Company.

By 1811 he reached the West Coast, although American traders had got there ahead of him, coming the other way by ship. Through Thompson the interior of what is now British Columbia was claimed for the North West Company. "Thus", he wrote, "I have fully completed the survey of this part of North America from sea to sea....the Maps of all have been drawn.... being now the work of twenty-seven years." He had mapped almost all the unknown areas of the West.

In 1812 Thompson retired to Montreal, where he could educate his children and work on refining his maps and journals. His greatest work consisted of 5 giant maps, each more than 3 by 9 feet, charting the West—the first reliable maps of the territory ever made.

Thompson died in 1857, his life ending as it had begun, in poverty. His work was not credited or published until 100 years later when another surveyor, James Tyrell, rediscovered it, made it known to the world, and wrote a biography of Thompson. Although at the time Mackenzie was better known (and richer), Thompson covered more territory, and passed on what he had learned to those who came after. For those struggling to found a new nation in the West, it was a priceless gift.

Mackenzie's journals may have whipped up interest in the great North West, and inspired the American president to send Lewis and Clark on their famous expedition. But it was Thompson's maps that helped pave the way. To Tyrell, his biographer, Thompson was "the greatest practical land geographer the world had produced". To Thompson himself he was, in his own words, just "a solitary traveller unknown to the world".

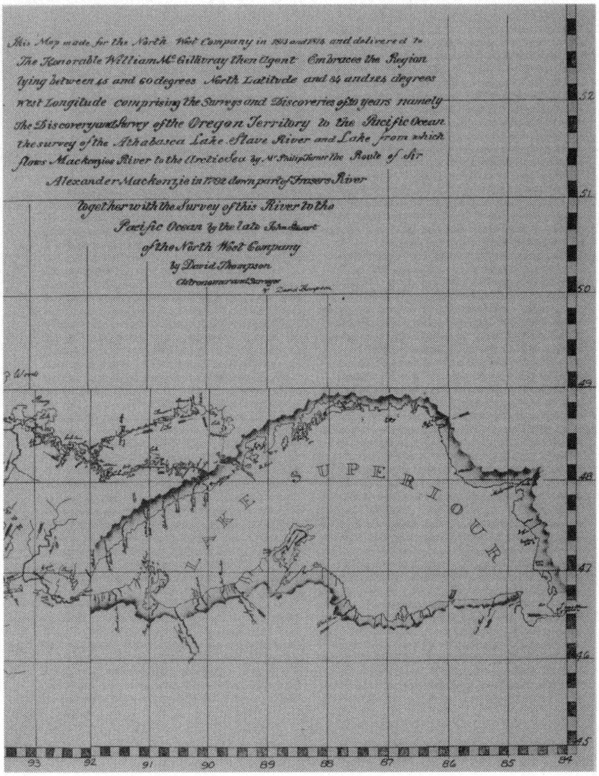

The beginning of Thompson's great map of the West, acknowledging his sponsors. It also includes a self-description as "astronomer and surveyor" and his (rather humble) signature. The map goes on (westerly) for ten feet and encompasses a million and a half square miles.

XXVI
The Selkirk Settlers

Thanks to people like Mackenzie and Thompson, the fur trade grew and spread. More traders spent winters with the natives and took native wives, and a new people—the Métis—developed and prospered on the prairies.

There was already fierce competition between the Hudson Bay Company and the North West Company. Tension and ill-will had been building for a long time, and anyone who wandered into the middle of the fight would be bound to suffer. Tragically, this turned out to be the Red River colonists, otherwise known as the Selkirk Settlers.

Thomas Douglas, the fifth earl of Selkirk, was well-educated, intelligent, kind, forward-looking, and ambitious. In the late 1700's when he was touring Scotland he was saddened to see the poor and discouraged tenant farmers being crowded out by sheep farming. Scottish landlords were starting to enclose and fence their properties, abolishing the ancient custom of common grazing lands and forcing tenants to find a living elsewhere – in cities or abroad. Selkirk wanted to help. He knew his own tenant farmers would eventually have to emigrate, so he set about finding them a good place to go.

He travelled around North America looking for somewhere to found a colony. Then, after reading Alexander Mackenzie's accounts, he was inspired by the romantic notion of settling the Red River plains. The idea of founding a colony suited Selkirk in several ways: it would be kind to give the Highlanders a new start; it would be a good political move for him; it would be a good place to try new agricultural techniques; and he might even make money.

The land Selkirk wanted was controlled by the Hudson Bay Company. So he bought up stock in the company and urged his friends to do the same. Soon Selkirk and his friends came to control a third of the HBC's shares, which gave him the influence to push his settlement plan.

Alexander Mackenzie thought the idea ridiculous. He had always said the area was unsuitable for agriculture and, worse, he knew that settlement would get in the way of the fur trade. In spite of this, Selkirk persuaded the HBC to sell him 300,000 square kilometres—five times the area of Scotland—for ten shillings.

Then began a propaganda war. Selkirk advertised all over Scotland for settlers and described the Red River area in most glowing and flattering terms, (he himself had never been there). Bishop Strachan of York, on the other hand, called it a "dreary wilderness" and said it was wicked to hold out false promises to the poor Highlanders, (he had never been there either). The truth, of course, lay somewhere in between. The land was lonely, hostile, given to flooding, with a punishing climate. But it was also very fertile, (though with a short growing season), and it was a large space where the Highlanders could make a new start.

The North West Company tried to discourage settlers and placed scary stories in all the Scottish newspapers, warning of Indian attacks. Miles Macdonell, the governor of the new colony, on the other hand, responded by travelling around Scotland telling Highlanders that Red River was the land of their dreams, the Promised Land.

In this way Macdonell managed to round up a boatload of settlers. The first group came over in 1812, and a second lot the next year. The Saulteaux natives were very friendly, not at all hostile, but settlement was still difficult. There were failed crops, hunger, and the usual fever and scurvy. Besides that the Métis, who lived in a settlement nearby and supplied buffalo meat to the North West Company, were not happy to have settlers there.

It was an awkward situation. Miles Macdonell, arrogant and bad-tempered, made it still more awkward. In 1814 he issued a proclamation that "no persons trading Furs or Provisions within the Territory...shall take out any provisions, either of flesh or game or vegetables." This meant that no food could be exported from Red River, the North West Company would not be able to supply its trading posts, and the Métis would be out of a job.

John Duncan Cameron of the North West Company predicted violence. He was convinced that Macdonell meant to drive the fur traders out of the district of Assiniboia. He urged the Métis to help drive out the settlers. At his suggestion the Métis put on war paint and pretended to be the Saulteaux. As one settler wrote:

"They immediately began to burn our houses in the daytime, and fire upon us during the night, saying the country was theirs. If we did not immediately quit the settlement, they would plunder us of our property, and burn the houses over our heads."

For a while the settlers found refuge in a Hudson Bay post at the north end of Lake Winnipeg. Later they returned to try and rebuild their colony. But worse was to come.

On June 19th, 1816, at Seven Oaks near the HBC's Red River trading post, twenty-five Hudson Bay employees and settlers rode out from Fort Douglas to meet sixty-one Métis who were riding by, wearing war paint. Words were exchanged, then a shot was fired, then more shots. No one knows who fired first. According to one survivor, almost all the settlers were either killed or wounded within a few minutes. When one of them ran toward the enemy to surrender he was shot through the head and sliced open with a knife. About 20 settlers were killed, and only one Métis, on that day which became known as the Massacre of Seven Oaks. As for the remaining settlers, their houses were destroyed. They surrendered and again retreated to the HBC post.

In reviewing this mess, a Canadian commission decided that it was a private war between rival fur trading companies, and blamed both sides. It was the bloodiest battle between the two companies and, happily, about the last. They were both exhausted.

In 1821 the Hudson Bay Company and the North West Company did what no one could have imagined— forced by the British government, they joined together as one company, under the Hudson Bay name. For the next forty years the company was governed by Sir George Simpson, a colourful character, efficient and tough, who entertained royalty with champagne and native pageants, and still found time to travel all over the country by canoe.

But even Simpson could not keep the fur trade going forever. By 1860 beaver hats had been replaced by silk, and the fur trade was changing and moving north (where it remained vital right into the 20th century).

The Red River colony, on the other hand, bounced back and prospered, though Selkirk did not live to see it. A census taken in 1822 counted 234 men, 161 women, 886 children, 126 houses and 160 gardens. The settlers had lived through floods, failed crops, locusts, scurvy, frostbite and murder. In the beginning they had lived on wild parsnips and nettles, and in the winter they were still wearing their English shoes. Yet thirty years later, a settler who had at first described the colony as "gloomy", now wrote "No farmers in the world, no settlement or colony of agriculturalists can be pronounced so happy, independent and comfortable as those in Red River."

This success unfortunately meant the end of the fur trade at Red River, just as Alexander Mackenzie had foretold. The North West Company's lifeline was being displaced by agriculture and settlement. As the fur trade declined in the south, so did the fortunes of the Métis. (Though later on many of them would move and establish themselves in the Mackenzie River and Peace River regions.) The industry that had started a new nation was dying.

Lord Selkirk as a young man

The Selkirk settlement

XXVII
Three Leaders and a Plague Ship

Revolution was in the air. At the beginning of the 19th century people all over the world, inspired by the ideals of the American and French Revolutions, were becoming militant in demanding liberty and justice.

The colonies of British North America by now had nearly a million people, and most of them were not happy with the fact that even the smallest decisions were made, not by themselves, but by people far away in London. Laws might be adopted by the colonial assemblies, but the colonial governors, appointed in London, held the only power to pass them. This meant there were always quarrels between the elected representatives of the people and an *un*elected government. People became angry, and soon began protesting in newspapers, criticizing their colonial rulers.

At York, the capital of Upper Canada, a Scottish immigrant named William Lyon Mackenzie published the "Colonial Advocate". In it he complained about the unprincipled, "narrow-minded and crafty" privileged few who influenced the governor and got him to do whatever they wanted, regardless of law. He called them the "Family Compact". In reply the attorney general of Upper Canada called Mackenzie a "reptile,... a conceited, red-headed fellow with an apron." Still the newspaper criticism continued.

In 1826 a gang of young men from some of the families Mackenzie was writing about destroyed his printing presses. Mackenzie, enraged, took the vandals to court, won his case, and was awarded enough money to replace the presses. This so lifted his spirits that he decided to go into politics.

In Halifax, Joseph Howe was busy with his own newspaper, the "Nova Scotian". Like Mackenzie, he saw Great Britain as being more democratic than its own colonies. But he had no wish to break from the mother country. "All we ask", he wrote, "is what exists at home in England—a system of responsibility to the people." Some of his criticisms about certain prominent local people got him into trouble. Nova Scotia's political leaders accused him of publishing seditious articles and took him to court. Howe acted in his own defence, saying that he hoped his accusers would become convinced "that they, and not I, are the real criminals here." The jury acquitted him. Like Mackenzie, his spirits and popularity were bolstered by the trial and he too entered politics.

In Lower Canada, the main opposition to the colonial government was the Parti Patriote. Their complaints were much the same as those in Upper Canada and Nova Scotia. They wanted to get rid of the legislative council appointed by the governor because it frequently rejected ideas put forward by the elected assembly. The leader of the Patriotes, Louis-Joseph Papineau, was a seigneur and a lawyer. He also happened to be the speaker of the House of Assembly. On one occasion when two journalists published attacks on the government they were thrown in jail for forty days. This caused Papineau to despair. He had begun as an admirer of the British parliamentary system, but now began to lean toward a republic, like the Americans. He even went so far as to predict that all of North America would eventually become republican.

While all this was going on, the population of the colonies was mushrooming. The economies of Europe had been shattered by the Napoleonic wars and many people, some of them deeply in debt, decided to emigrate to a new land with new opportunities. In the early 1830s the number of people coming every year through Quebec, the port of entry, was greater then the number of people already living there. This growing population meant, for one thing, that there would be more people to voice complaints against the government. Many of them began to ask their governors for better roads and schools, but were ignored. This added to a growing list of grievances.

While Upper Canada was growing the fastest, Lower Canada still had more people—almost 400,000. There the English and French lived in separate districts, with separate languages and religions, but got along peacefully enough, for the most part. (In fact the governor's wife, Louise Aylmer, was friends with the Papineaus and with Monseigneur Lartigue, the Bishop of Montreal—she actually preferred the society of French Canadians).

In the countryside, tenant farmers lived under the seigneurial system, as they had for some two hundred years. But land was becoming scarce. The landowners, both French and English, kept putting rents higher and higher so that the young habitants either had to find land farther and farther away, or else abandon farming and find work in the city. Resentment was growing and there began to be protests.

Politics in Lower Canada were already tricky. The English Party was made up of English, Scots and Americans. The Parti Patriote was mostly French Canadians plus some Irish, who distrusted the British. During elections both parties sometimes sent thugs to disrupt the voting so that polling stations had to be closed. On May 21st, 1832, after a polling station was shut down, supporters of the English Party began heckling a group of Patriotes. A fight broke out; the military was called in to keep order, and they began firing into the crowd. Three Canadiens were shot. The day after that it was announced that the Parti Patriote had won the election by 4 votes.

Louis-Joseph-Papineau was terribly upset. He wrote to his friend Lord Aylmer, the governor general: "My heart is racked with pain, and my letter will find you in the same situation....The troops sent to protect His Majesty's subjects shot them. No such tragedy has ever before afflicted Canada."

In Quebec the Parti Patriote had held a majority in the House of Assembly for many years, but they were growing tired of their demands always being ignored and blocked by the governor and his appointees. In 1834 they drew up a list of claims and grievances called the "92 Resolutions", and took it all the way to London. In this document they claimed that the secretary of state for the colonies had not given the colonies the British constitutional rights that had been promised. They even hinted that they might like to join the United States instead.

The English Party was alarmed by the tone of the "92 Resolutions", and by the Patriote win in the 1834 elections. A powerful Montreal businessman, John Molson, lashed out at the Patriotes in a public meeting; he criticized the seigneurial system as corrupt and fit only to be thrown on the garbage heap. The hatred expressed was so violent that the French began to fear that the British were out to crush them.

In the same year, 1834, the town of York, Upper Canada, was renamed Toronto. William Lyon Mackenzie, as well as being a newspaper publisher, was now the Mayor. Like Papineau in Lower Canada, he also drafted a list of demands and sent it to London. It was called the "Seventh Report on Grievances" and was severely critical of the government of Upper Canada.

In Nova Scotia Joseph Howe, now a member of the House of Assembly, continued to write much the same things in his newspaper the "Nova Scotian". He pointed out that the King in Britain had less power than his own representatives in the colonies. Howe said he still had no wish to cut off ties to Britain, but that he did want to live and die enjoying the same constitutional rights that British subjects in the Mother Country took for granted.

In the midst of all these troubles, there was the plague. At the beginning of June, 1832, a ship had come over from Ireland and landed in Quebec. Several of the immigrants on board had complained of fever. Three days later the first cholera victim was dead and the disease spread like a fire out of control—to Montreal, then to Upper Canada, through the crowded shanty towns of the poor. The lack of sewage and garbage collection led to water contamination, and hundreds died each day. Newspaper articles tried to keep down the panic by advising people to consult doctors and pharmacists who "have the necessary remedies and their prices are within the reach of everyone." This, of course, was not true. Doctors were overwhelmed and helpless. They believed in those days that cholera was transmitted by fumes in the air; so to purify the air English officers tried firing cannon, and sanitary officials tried burning tar. By the end of the year 9,000 people were dead, more than half of them in Lower Canada. Fear and panic had reached such a pitch that there were even rumours that the British had somehow caused the epidemic on purpose.

All this death, anger and blame did nothing to calm the developing political crisis. By 1837 it was clear that this stewpot of troubles was coming to the boil. It would not take much now for the pot to boil over.

Toronto, 1835

XXVIII
Rebellion

The year 1837 did not start out well. For one thing, in Lower Canada there had been several years of poor crops and the people were feeling desperate and defeated. The "Canadian" newspaper reported: "...that some habitants have taken to eating their own horses....Many habitants don't have even a potato....The ones who are better off barely have enough to get by....It is certain that most of them will die of hunger if relief is not provided."

The other thing was that London had rejected the "Ninety-Two Resolutions". The British government was afraid that if they gave the Patriotes what they asked for, Britain would lose its hold over its North American colonies. The authorities in Lower Canada were more afraid of the Patriotes, and began to strengthen their military defences.

Indeed, there was clear warning of revolt. The habitants of the Richelieu Valley began to use an old custom called the "charivari" to show their discontent. This was a violent demonstration in which people would surround the house of someone they disapproved of and make a deafening, frightening NOISE, using any kind of noisemaker they could lay hands on. During that summer the tactic was used on people who refused to join the Patriotes, justices of the peace, and other representatives of the Crown.

In October there was a big meeting in the Richelieu Valley. Five thousand people assembled under the red, white and green flag of the Parti Patriote to hear their most powerful speaker, Louis Joseph Papineau.

As the great man walked up to the rostrum, five thousand voices cheered and the militia fired a volley in his honour. Then Papineau spoke: "Fellow citizens! Brothers who share our suffering! All of you, whatever your origin, your language or your religion, to whom equal laws and the rights of man are precious, we call on you to take that position which....will bring respect for yourselves and success for your demands—organizing in your respective parishes and townships." He boldly urged them to elect their own justices of the peace. This was the farthest he had ever gone. He knew he was defying the most powerful empire on earth. But even this was not bold enough for Dr. Wolfred Nelson, the speaker of the assembly. "The time has come," he said, "to melt down our dishes and tin spoons to make bullets!" The crowd erupted with more and louder cheers.

That same day in the Place des Armes in Montreal Peter McGill, the president of the Bank of Montreal, addressed a different crowd of demonstrators. He warned that any acts of rebellion would be an outrage to peaceful citizens and would not be tolerated.

In Upper Canada Mackenzie, who supported the Patriotes, was carrying on his own campaign for reform, with fiery speeches directed at people who were not satisfied with the way they were being treated. Soon Mackenzie's supporters began to conduct military drills.

Obviously rebellion was now unavoidable and everyone would have to take sides. The Bishop of Montreal warned the Patriotes, asking them if they had thought seriously about the horrors and suffering that a civil war would bring. Nobody listened.

Back in Toronto the lieutenant governor was aware of trouble brewing, but decided that the situation was worse in Lower Canada. He sent all the British troops stationed in Upper Canada to Lower Canada. By the end of year not one single regular soldier remained in Upper Canada.

That was when the countryside of Lower Canada exploded. Not only were the Patriotes planning to declare independence for Lower Canada, they were going about with guns terrorizing everyone, including justices of the peace, who had refused to join them. The British thought that if they allowed the revolutionists to arm and did nothing to stop them, they would lose the province. So it became important for the military to arrest the leaders. The army was sent in.

The commander of the British troops was General Colborne. Unluckily for the Patriotes, he was not just any colonial officer, but an experienced strategist who had fought with Wellington against Napoleon. Colborne ordered a raid on the Patriote leaders' headquarters in the Richelieu Valley. Five companies of soldiers were sent to St. Charles, five other companies to

St. Denis. Their orders were to take over the villages, then move on to the armed Patriote camp in St. Charles.

The rebels were waiting for them. As the soldiers approached, church bells were heard ringing the alarm. Patriotes ran out from a stone house and began firing from behind a barricade. The soldiers took shelter behind a stone wall. Thus began the battle of St. Denis.

Dr. Wolfred Nelson was in charge of defending St. Denis. He led 800 men, ordinary citizens, very determined and probably rather nervous. Col. Charles Gore led the 300 British troops. Combat went on for six hours with little gain on either side until, in the middle of the afternoon, reinforcements came to St. Denis from other villages. The British soldiers were tired from the long march earlier in the day, and they were running out of ammunition. They hadn't expected so much resistance. Finally Col. Gore ordered a retreat. At the end of the day 12 British soldiers and 13 Patriotes lay dead.

The Patriotes celebrated their victory, but Dr. Nelson was in a more thoughtful mood. He knew they had merely won a skirmish—now the war would begin in earnest. It was at this point that the lieutenant governor of Upper Canada, Sir Francis Bond Head, received a letter from General Colborne saying, "The Civil War has now commenced", and asking him to send troops to Montreal.

On November 25th Lieut.-Col. George Wetherall, with 425 men, attacked St. Charles. The 250 Patriotes, positioned behind a barricade, knew the fate of their rebellion was at stake. But this time they were only 250 poorly equipped and inexperienced men, against one of the toughest regiments in the British army. The Patriotes—men, women, children and the elderly—all tried to do their share in the defence. Even the women cast bullets and made cartridges. The men on the barricades kept up a steady fire on the British line. Then the British troops were ordered to advance with fixed bayonets, pushing the rebels into the freezing Richelieu River. According to the only surviving account, the Patriotes were kneeling in the water waiting for the soldiers, with their rifles upside down as if to signal surrender. Then at the last moment they opened fire. The soldiers, enraged, yelled their war cry and charged. It was a slaughter.

There was no Patriote victory this time as there had been at St. Denis. By the end of this day 3 British soldiers and 150 Patriotes lay dead on the battle field. Louis-Joseph Papineau, and hundreds of other Patriotes, made for the United States border.

It didn't take long for the news to reach the ears of William Lyon Mackenzie in Upper Canada. By this time, since all the British troops had gone from Toronto to Montreal, Mackenzie thought it a good moment to seize power and form a provisional government. He rounded up supporters, especially disenchanted farmers from the villages near Toronto, and told them to report to Montgomery's Tavern north of Toronto, bringing whatever guns they possessed.

On December 4th they assembled, tired, hungry and disorganized. The next day they marched down Yonge Street. All the soldiers might have gone from the city, but the faithful militia was still there waiting for the rebels. Shots were exchanged back and forth. The rebels' system of fighting was for the front line to fire, then instead of stepping aside, to fall flat on their faces to allow the next line of men behind them to fire. Many of the country folk, seeing this and hearing the rifle shots, thought the fallen men were killed. They turned and ran.

The encounter two days later was a bit better organized—on both sides. A thousand militia and volunteers were given weapons and ammunition and ordered to drive the rebels out of Montgomery's Tavern. Mackenzie's men were waiting for them along Yonge Street, but there were only 400 of them left, only half of them with guns; the other half were armed with pick-axes. The rebels began to shoot at the oncoming militia, but when their fire was returned by a thunderous barrage of artillery, they were so startled that they dropped their weapons and took to their heels. The battle lasted only a few minutes. After that the militia burned Montgomery's Tavern to the ground, and the rebellion in Upper Canada was over.

In Lower Canada martial law was declared in the district of Montreal, so things were quiet again. Only one Patriote stronghold was left—the county of Deux Montagnes. Rather than attacking directly, Colborne staged a slow and stately parade along the Chemin du Roi in St. Eustache before a crowd of onlookers: first came the infantry, the artillery, the cavalry, and the general staff in brilliant uniforms, commanded by Sir John Colborne himself; then the war machines, cannons, and large red carriages for transporting the wounded. Most Patriotes saw this, realized they had no hope of winning, and fled. The 250 that remained holed up in a church. Colborne ordered the church to be bombarded, but it was so solidly built that it withstood two hours of cannon ball fire. Then the soldiers tried driving the rebels out of their hiding place in the loft but couldn't get at them, and met with such heavy rifle fire that as a last resort they set fire to the altar cloth. The fear of fire finally drove the Patriotes out, and the battle ended. Seventy Patriotes and three soldiers were dead. After that the soldiers and volunteers went about the county of Deux Montagnes burning the villages and houses of rebel leaders. Hundreds of Patriotes, including Dr. Wolfred Nelson, tried to reach the American border but were taken prisoner. Louis-Joseph Papineau remained in exile in Albany.

In Upper Canada, sometime later, many of the rebels were caught also trying to flee to the United States. Two were hanged, most were given amnesty after a few months in prison. As for William Lyon Mackenzie, he escaped to Buffalo, New York, with a price on his head.

XXIX
Lord Durham

The British government had had enough of all this fighting; they decided to take action to end it. In the spring of 1838 they sent a new governor general to lead an enquiry into the rebellion.

John George Lambton, first Earl of Durham, was a youngish aristocrat and a fine diplomat, comfortable with all kinds of people, from the workers in his father's coal mines to the lords and ladies at court and in the great houses of London.

The first thing he did on becoming governor general was to write a proclamation to the people of the colonies: "I beg you to consider me as a friend and arbitrator, ready at all times to listen to your wishes, complaints and grievances, and fully determined to act with the strictest impartiality."

The next thing he did was to grant amnesty to the Patriotes. To celebrate the day of Queen Victoria's coronation 150 Patriotes were freed, and eight rebels, including Dr. Wolfred Nelson, were exiled to Bermuda. "Not one drop of blood has been shed", wrote Durham to Queen Victoria, "the guilty have received justice, the misguided mercy".

But not all was calm and secure. At the same time that Durham was going on with his enquiry, another rebellion was being plotted. It was organized and led by two radicals: Wolfred Nelson's brother Robert, a Montreal surgeon, and Chevalier de Lorimier, an idealistic young notary. (Papineau would have no more to do with the rebellion which he thought was doomed to failure). This new group of Patriotes had formed a secret society called the "Société des frères chasseurs", rather like a lodge of the Freemasons. For the initiation ritual the novice got down on his knees, blindfolded, and surrounded by his comrades. He then swore an oath on the bible:

"I solemnly swear, freely and before almighty God, to observe the secret and mysterious signs of the Society of Hunters, to obey all the rules and regulations the Society may establish.....failing which I consent to my property being destroyed and my own neck severed to the bone." Then the blindfold was taken off.

In the fall of 1838, meanwhile, Lord Durham was forced to resign. (It seems he had overstepped his legal authority in exiling the Patriote leaders to Bermuda, which was not a penal colony). So the field was left to the military, and to the dreaded General Colborne.

That same fall the Frères chasseurs invaded from the United States and there was an uprising in Lower Canada. They attacked the seigneurial manor of Beauharnais belonging to Edward Ellice, one of the richest landowners in Lower Canada. In less than an hour 300 Frères chasseurs took over the manor and kidnapped 60 villagers, including Ellice's son and daughter-in-law. The family was treated well though, and freed after less than a week.

The rebellion really ran out of steam when the expected guns and ammunition from the United States were stopped at the border. The rebels lost heart and again flocked to the U.S. border seeking asylum. The Glengarry Highlanders, 1000 strong, went about burning the whole Beauharnais region. The army and volunteers, supported by the authorities, did the same to the region south of Montreal. The innocent and the guilty were equally terrorized. As one journalist described the scene: "All the country back of La Prairie presented the frightful spectacle of a vast expanse of livid flame." Because of all this torching of property Sir John Colborne was nicknamed "old firebrand".

By now both Papineau and Mackenzie, still in exile in the U.S., had given up on the idea of armed rebellion. But in Upper Canada, American adventurers sympathetic to the cause kept it going a bit longer. They staged border raids (without the approval of the American government) until in September of 1838 they were captured by the Canadian militia at Windsor, and that was the end of that.

Afterwards, in 1838 and 1839, hundreds of rebels were convicted of high treason. In Upper Canada 17 men were executed; in Lower Canada 12 were hanged, including Chevalier de Lorimier. In the fall of 1839 more than 130 prisoners from Upper and Lower Canada were sent to the prison colony of Australia.

Now it seemed that all this death and destruction, not to mention twenty years of work for parliamentary reform, were for nothing. In Lower Canada there was no constitution, for the time being, and instead of an assembly, a special council appointed by the governor general ruled the colony.

Meanwhile, back in London, Lord Durham wrote "A Report on the Affairs of British North America". Like Papineau, Mackenzie and Howe, Durham believed that harmony could be restored *only* by giving the people more, not less, influence on their own government. He also saw a serious problem for Lower Canada: "I expected to find a contest between a government and a people: I found two nations warring in a single state." He saw that the "deadly animosity" that divided the French and the English would have to be stopped. He proposed to unite the two Canadas.

The government in London refused to make the colonial parliament more democratic; they feared this would mean the end of the empire. Still, they approved the idea of uniting the two Canadas.

Lord Durham did not live to see his dream for Canada become reality. Eighteen months later he died of tuberculosis. He was only forty-eight.

XXX
The Reformers
Part 1

Lord Durham had done all he could. Now Joseph Howe in Halifax took up the cry:

"The principle of responsibility (to the people) must be introduced into all the colonies without delay", he wrote, urging London to support the Durham Report. "It is the only simple and safe remedy for....a very common disease."

Once again his opinions got him in trouble with certain prominent local people. When he printed an unfavourable comparison between the sons of the rich and some of his young apprentices, a certain rich parent, claiming he had been insulted, challenged Howe—this time to a duel.

The opponent shot first; he missed. Then Howe, instead of shooting back, raised his pistol and fired into the air. "I never intended to fire at him," Howe later claimed. He had only wanted to teach them a lesson in coolness and moderation. Anyway, "All's well that ends well," he said.

Far to the west (which to people in Nova Scotia at that time meant Toronto), new men were taking up the cause of democracy. The new leader of the Reformers was a young lawyer named Robert Baldwin. He was a big, slow-moving man, a former student of Dr. Strachan, the Anglican bishop of Toronto. In the 1837 rebellion Baldwin had tried to bring together William Lyon Mackenzie and the lieutenant governor, Sir Francis Bond Head. Now he wanted to bring the Reformers from Upper and Lower Canada together. He knew that the support of French Canadians was needed to win a majority in the new assembly of United Canada.

Louis-Hippolyte La Fontaine, in the absence of the exiled Patriote leaders, had become one of the most powerful politicians in Lower Canada. He was a young man of thirty-two who looked a lot like Napoleon (and cultivated a similar hairstyle in order to emphasize the likeness). Like Baldwin in Upper Canada, he had tried to bring together the Patriote leaders and the colonial government, also without success. Baldwin wrote to him, "There is, and must be, no question of races....The Reformers of Upper Canada are resolved to unite with their Lower Canadian Brethren...cordially and as friends." La Fontaine replied, "It is in the interest of both provinces to meet...in a spirit of peace, union, friendship and brotherhood. United action is needed now more than ever."

In February of 1841 the new constitution came into effect. The capital of the United Province of Canada was Kingston. In the assembly the two former provinces, Upper and Lower Canada, had the same number of representatives, even though Lower Canada had a larger population. This was a ploy to ensure that the French Canadians didn't have more political clout than the English. It also made it hard for the Reformers. They needed each other in order to form a majority in the assembly.

In the first election after the rebellions the Conservatives, by using tricks like moving electoral boundaries and placing polling stations far away from French villages, tried very hard to prevent the Reformers from winning. There was mob violence and the army was called in. Later on Baldwin and La Fontaine helped each other to get elected in each other's ridings. For years they worked together toward democratic government, and became not only political allies but great friends as well.

But *still* London refused to grant autonomy to her North American colonies.

In the meantime there came more misery in the form of yet another outbreak of plague. In the spring of 1847 a ship, the first of many, brought a load of 241 immigrants escaping from the Great Famine in Ireland. They anchored off Grosse-Ile, an island where immigrants with typhus, cholera and smallpox were quarantined. One immigrant wrote on his diary about "helpless creatures being carried by sailors over the rocks on their way to the hospital", boats arriving with dying patients and another long line of boats carrying the dead to the burial ground, like "an endless funeral procession". During that terribly hot summer fifty people died each day at

Grosse-Ile. By the end of the year, twenty thousand Irish immigrants had died.

The Great Famine in Ireland had another effect. Up to now Britain had operated under a system of what were called "preferential tariffs". This meant that the colonies were given easier access to the British market than other countries, without having to pay as much. It also meant higher food prices. Because the victims of famine needed food, lots of it and at lower prices, Britain finally abandoned these colonial preferences. Now that the colonies were no longer in a special trading position, there was no good reason for Britain to control their domestic politics. The government in London adopted free trade, which was what many in Britain had wanted anyway.

So London finally granted to the Reformers of British North America what they had been struggling for over decades: self-government. Lord Grey, the colonial secretary, in a letter to the lieutenant-governor of Nova Scotia, wrote "It is neither possible nor desirable to carry on the government of any of the British provinces of North America in opposition to the opinion of its inhabitants". In other words, autonomy was here to stay.

Joseph Howe's big moment had come. Early in 1848 his party won a general election and took power in Nova Scotia. This was the first freely elected colonial government within the British Empire.

In United Canada the Reformers, led of course by Robert Baldwin and Louis-Hippolyte La Fontaine, did likewise. Baldwin spoke for both La Fontaine and himself when he declared, "The Province has passed through a long and arduous struggle for the establishment of a system of government founded on the broad basis of British constitutional principles...The battle has been fought. The victory has been achieved."

The same year Louis-Joseph Papineau, who had returned to Canada after being granted amnesty, was elected to represent St. Maurice, and tried to undo the Union. But it was a different world now, the time of the Patriotes was over, and most people now supported La Fontaine. Papineau left public life and retired to his manor in the country. By now almost all the old rebels had been granted amnesty. In 1849 William Lyon Mackenzie was the last to be allowed back.

Lafontaine

Thomas D'arcy McGee

XXXI
The Reformers
Part 2

British North America now had more than 2 million people. It seemed to be prosperous and running smoothly. But in Toronto, Montreal and Halifax, businessmen were worried.

Britain's new free trade policy had indeed left the colonies free to govern themselves, as the government in London was no longer interested in controlling their domestic policy. But it also meant that the colonies were losing business to foreigners who could supply English industry with cheaper raw materials. Jobs were scarce, and getting scarcer.

In the meantime the parliament of United Canada had moved from Kingston to Montreal. Then came a new political crisis. The Baldwin-La Fontaine government wanted to compensate people in Lower Canada for property lost during the rebellion. But since many of these people were the same ones who had fought against the government, some thought that giving them compensation would be like rewarding treason. Some English even thought it would be like rewarding the French just because they were French.

In the spring of 1849 Durham's son-in-law, Lord Elgin, became the new governor general. He faced a dilemma. On one hand, if he did not accept the Rebellion Losses Bill, as it was called, he would be going against the principles of responsible government for which his father-in-law had fought so hard. On the other hand, if he did accept the bill he would have most of the English people in Montreal angry with him.

He chose responsible government. The result was that the English were indeed angry with him. They felt betrayed. When Elgin left the assembly building an angry crowd pelted his carriage with rotten eggs. The Montreal "Gazette" for April 25th, 1849, stirred up emotions even further with the headlines:

"Disgrace of Great Britain....

Canada Sold and Given Away!

Rebellion Losses Bill Passed."

This was followed by "A Mass Meeting will be held on the Place d'Armes this evening at 8 o'clock. Anglo-Saxons to the struggle, now is your time."

That evening the crowd was whipped up into a frenzy. A mob gathered around the parliament building and, while members were still sitting and the house was full of spectators, set out to destroy it. They began by breaking windows and doors. Then someone jumped onto the Speaker's chair and shouted "I dissolve Parliament." Someone else set fire to the gas pipes in several places and soon the whole building, including rare paintings, provincial records, acts of Parliament, the library—all went up in flames. The members barely escaped with their lives. Destruction and chaos reigned.

In this atmosphere it was easy for some people in the opposition to take advantage of the situation and stir up old feelings—of loyalists against rebels, English against French. There was even talk of joining the United States.

Joseph Howe in Nova Scotia was horrified to learn of these events. He declared that if keeping Canada British meant behaving this way or causing any kind of injustice to the French half of the population (who were after all British subjects), then he would have nothing to do with it.

The English in the rest of United Canada, however, did not support the Montreal Tories, and La Fontaine's united party, combined with the support of the Church, was too strong. In the end sanity prevailed.

Two years later, in 1851, Robert Baldwin retired to his property north of Toronto and took up gardening. Political struggle had exhausted him. Shortly afterward his friend Louis-Hippolyte La Fontaine also left politics to practise law.

William Lyon Mackenzie returned from exile and was elected to the parliament of United Canada. Again he tried writing newspaper articles about political corruption, but now nobody was interested. He gave up, retired in 1859, and died soon afterward.

Louis-Joseph Papineau lived quietly with his wife Julie on their seigneury in the Ottawa Valley. He died when he was 85, the only one of these four to live to a ripe old age.

Joseph Howe was the only one to continue in politics. He had already steered Nova Scotia into becoming the first colony in the British Empire to gain responsible government. Now he took up a new cause in the building of a new country—the railway.

"I will venture to predict", he said in 1851, "that in five or six years we shall make the journey hence to Quebec and Montreal, and home through Portland and St. John, by rail; and I believe that many....will live to hear the whistle of the steam engine in the passes of the Rocky Mountains, and to make the journey from Halifax to the Pacific in five or six days."

George Brown

Georges-Etienne Cartier

XXXII
Confederation?

The British North American settlements in the 1860's were a strange assortment, strung out all the way across the continent from east to west. Much of the vast northwestern territory was still held by the Hudson Bay Company; but the United Stated had their sights set on these great plains which were sparsely inhabited by native tribes, Métis and fur traders. On the other side of the Rocky Mountains, British Columbia was having a gold rush which was attracting thousands of Americans. Away off to the east was Newfoundland, all by itself and surrounded by the Atlantic Ocean. The separate colonies of Prince Edward Island, New Brunswick and Nova Scotia were some distance apart and rarely spoke to each other. And in the middle of it all, with its two peoples, two languages and two religions, sat the large, ungainly United Province of Canada.

The men who would eventually bring together these bits and pieces into one nation were themselves a strange assortment. They were different not only in the regions they came from but also in religion, politics, interests and, of course, personality. The strangest thing of all was that all four of these men had at some time in their lives distrusted, argued with, or fought against the British colonial administration.

John Alexander Macdonald was born a Highland Scot but came to Canada at the age of five.

When he was just fifteen he articled with a Kingston lawyer and eventually became a lawyer himself, and the most prominent politician in Upper Canada. He was a witty, charming man with a gift for organizing and great energy and determination. Tall and gangly, with a shock of dark hair and a bulbous nose, it was said he could wind anyone—man, woman or child—around his little finger. It was also said that he drank too much. For fourteen years he was married to his first cousin, Isabella Clark, who was ill for most of that time. She died in 1857, leaving him with one surviving son.

George Etienne Cartier was the chief politician of the French in Lower Canada. He too began his career as a lawyer, fought in the 1837 rebellion at the battle of St. Denis, and fled to the United States for six months before returning to Montreal. At the age of 34 he became a member of United Canada's Legislative Assembly. He was a fine orator and he once spoke in Parliament, criticizing the government, for thirteen hours straight. He was fond of champagne and singing at parties, making everyone join in.

Cartier and Macdonald became friends and allies (rather like La Fontaine and Baldwin before) and helped each other. Although they were of different races and religions, they shared a common conservative view of how Canada should grow and how religious differences could be resolved. Soon they formed a political alliance.

George Brown was a different matter. He disapproved of the Macdonald-Cartier alliance and everything about them, including their fondness for alcohol. He was a huge (6'4") dour Scot, a liberal Protestant, who thought all Conservatives were corrupt, and was suspicious of all Roman Catholics. He once called Cartier "that damnable little French Canadian". The population of Upper Canada was now greater than that of Lower Canada, and Brown felt that Upper Canada should have more votes then Lower Canada. (He had been less keen on representation by population when Lower Canada had more people). On one occasion when he made fun of Macdonald in his newspaper The Globe, Macdonald replied that voters "would rather have a drunken John A. Macdonald than a sober George Brown". In 1851 Brown was elected to Parliament, so the voters got both.

Thomas D'Arcy McGee was an Irish Catholic editor, journalist and poet. He moved to North America as a young man, first to Boston and later to Montreal where, in 1857, he started a newspaper and was elected to the legislative assembly. He and George Brown did not get along. McGee was insistent that Canada needed to get rid of those divisions of race and religion that stood in the way. "The man who says this cannot be done is a blockhead", he wrote.

In the meantime the Civil War was raging in the United States. There was threat of invasion from south of the border, but at first the only invasion was by immigrants, draft dodgers, refugees from the Union army, and escaped slaves. The British government was tired of spending money for the defence of its North American colonies. Some of the British troops were sent home.

But by 1864 the Civil War was ending, there was renewed fear of invasion from the south, and the British territories were not well defended. To protect itself British North America needed to be united. A way had to be found, and quickly.

Miraculously, George Brown did the unimaginable. He joined forces with his enemies, the "Corruptionists" Cartier and Macdonald. Together they formed a coalition government whose one and only purpose was to unify the colonies.

McGee admired what Brown had done. As he wrote, "Brown has given the greatest exhibition of moral courage I ever knew. Next to him the man who has taken the greatest risk to his political career is Cartier". Indeed Cartier was criticized in Lower Canada for joining this alliance, as the French were well aware of Brown's anti-French views. However, Cartier saw that a federation would have a number of advantages for everyone. While the new federal government would have power over defence and foreign trade, the provinces would control their own schools. There would no longer be religious conflicts because Upper Canadian Protestants and Lower Canadian Catholics would no longer have anything to do with each other's school systems.

Cartier was also connected to railroad and banking interests. He saw that a larger country would offer more economic opportunities, and people would not have to go across the border to New England's factories to find work. The prospect of new markets in the west and new jobs in Montreal's railway shops might make people want a confederation.

Governor General Monck took this opportunity to promote the idea in the Maritime provinces as well. The Lieutenant Governor of New Brunswick, Arthur Gordon, was already enthusiastic. A conference was planned to discuss the idea, and Monck invited the Canadians (Upper and Lower) to come too. The date was set for September 1st, 1864, in Charlottetown, Prince Edward Island.

Brown, Macdonald, McGee and Alexander Galt, businessman, finance minister and railway man, travelled together to Prince Edward Island on the steamer "Queen Victoria". The weather was fine, they were in a festive mood, and there was a great deal of champagne on board. When they arrived in Charlottetown the good mood continued. There were rousing and persuasive speeches from all the delegates, accompanied by lobster lunches, picnics, balls (and more champagne). By the end of the talks everyone was delighted by the idea of a new union. It wasn't to be just a Maritime union. Little Prince Edward Island had become the birthplace of a much bigger idea: Canadian Confederation.

But they still hadn't settled on the terms that would satisfy everyone. For this difficult political task the delegates agreed to meet again the next month—in Quebec.

John A. MacDonald

John A. MacDonald - an early photo in a locket

The Charlottetown Conference

XXXIII
The Quebec Conference

The thirty-three delegates to Quebec arrived in October of 1864, in the middle of a snowstorm. The hotel where most of them stayed was also full of railway men who were naturally very interested in what was going on. This was the great age of railways, symbol of the Industrial Revolution, and railways were changing the world. Some of these railway builders and investors saw in Confederation a great new opportunity, and had ambitions to expand west to the Pacific. Cartier himself had railway interests. He benefited politically from the fact that trains were manufactured in Montreal, supplying jobs. He was also the lawyer for the Grand Trunk Railway, which benefited him financially. In those days nobody seemed to worry about conflicts of interest.

The meetings in Quebec were carried on in secret. The press was not allowed in and only the delegates took notes. Macdonald took the lead and pushed for a strong central government, which would have certain powers while the provinces kept others. In fact he did a lot of the actual work on the constitution by himself, drafting 50 of the 72 resolutions. He was the only one there with a background in constitutional law. He remarked that whatever was good, or bad, in the Constitution was due to him.

Representation by population in the House of Commons was, of course, decided on. It was proposed that the Senate should be made up of three equal blocks of seats, one for each of Upper Canada, Lower Canada, and the Maritimes (the four Atlantic provinces). There were some arguments from the Maritimes that in playing by these rules the smaller provinces would lose out to the larger ones. With all the arguing and negotiating, the delegates found the easiest way to describe what they wanted in a new country was to describe what they didn't like in the United States model.

In Macdonald's words, "The great evil in the United States is that the President is a despot for four years", but under the British Constitution the people retain power through Parliament, "and are free from such despotism".

Adding to the confusion and exhaustion of the delegates during these proceedings were the weeks of late-night parties and balls and the never-ending flow of wine. According to one observer, "The festivities interfere somewhat with the progress of business," and one of the delegates prayed "that we may be removed from this dear, charming, abominable, killing, pleasure-ridden city".

While all this was going on a telegram arrived at Quebec. It said that a group of Confederate soldiers, pretending to be Canadians on a fishing holiday, had been robbing banks in Vermont. They had then turned around and fled to Canada. President Lincoln stopped the posse of angry Americans who wanted to storm across the border into Canada to retrieve the money from the thieves. Governor General Monck ordered out the militia and several of the thieves were caught and tried in court. But they got off on a technicality and, worse, got to keep the money. This incident caused hostility and distrust on both sides of the border. Canadians would now have to produce passports before they could enter the United States; Monck sent out troops to police the border.

Canada now had a better reason than ever to unite. The delegates at the conference at last agreed on terms, which were then adopted. These were known as the Quebec Resolutions. The tone of these Resolutions was deliberately different from the kind of revolutionary phrases France and America had used in the century before. Instead it was written as a sober, reliable contract, promising "peace, order and good government".

Brown wrote that night to his wife: "Conference through at six o'clock this evening—constitution adopted—a most creditable document...".

XXXIV
Selling an Idea

The happy results of the Quebec Conference did not mean that Confederation seemed a good idea to *everyone*. In Nova Scotia Charles Tupper was now the head of government, but Joseph Howe, still beloved and influential, was against it. "Did anyone ever propose to unite Scotland with Poland or Hungary?—inland countries 800 miles off in the heart of Europe?" he wrote in the Halifax Chronicle.

To Premier Tilley of New Brunswick Confederation did not seem so absurd. He was keen on the idea, as well as on a railroad to pull it all together. But just at the wrong moment he lost an election and was replaced by people who were very much against Confederation. As for Prince Edward Island and Newfoundland, they soundly rejected the Quebec Resolutions.

The idea of Confederation was not entirely safe in Upper and Lower Canada either. Macdonald and Cartier were for it, of course, but Anton-Aimé Dorion, leader of the opposing "Rouges", thought that Confederation would not be good for French Canadians. Here again the Catholic Church stepped in, this time to help persuade the people to support Cartier and Confederation.

Finally the Quebec Resolutions were voted on in Parliament and passed, 91 to 33. Among the French majority in Lower Canada (now referred to as Canada East) the vote for and against was roughly fifty-fifty. The thing that swung the vote in the Maritimes was another threat from the United States, this time from the Fenians.

The Fenians were actually a more real danger in Upper Canada. In early June of 1866 thousands of them crossed the river from Buffalo and clashed with a volunteer militia at Ridgeway. Ten volunteers were killed and thirty-eight wounded. Again in the spring of 1867 the Fenians threatened, but their invasions never came to much. Their main effect was the same as in the Maritimes—to give everyone a good scare and a push toward union.

Macdonald and his colleagues now had the plan for Confederation ready to go. All that remained was to get the British North America bill passed. For that purpose the Confederation team, which included Macdonald, Cartier, Brown and Alexander Galt, travelled to London. According to an observer in the Colonial Office where they presented the first draft of their bill, "Macdonald was the ruling genius and spokesman". He skilfully steered a course between the wishes of the French and of the English, with diplomacy and a "cool, ready fluency" in arguing the case.

The question was also raised of what to call this new country. It was neither a kingdom nor a republic. Tilley of New Brunswick, who read the Bible everyday, quoted part of a psalm: "His dominion shall be also from sea to sea". So it was decided to call the new country a Dominion.

It took a long time for the British North America bill to go through the British House of Commons, then the House of Lords, as well as several delays. During the long wait Macdonald had time for several adventures. The worst was when he awoke one night to find that his bed was on fire. (*Surely* he had not been smoking in bed!) He hurried next door to Cartier's room to get help and luckily escaped with fairly minor injuries. The best adventure: While roaming about London as a tourist with the other delegates, he ran into an old friend, Agnes Bernard, whom he had known ten years before after his first wife's death. They had always enjoyed each other's company and this time, after a brief courtship, Agnes agreed to be his wife. They were married in London, in St. George's church in Hanover Square, by the bishop of Montreal.

The British North America bill was finally signed by Queen Victoria on March 29th, 1867. Macdonald and the other delegates went home to Canada. On July 1 at noon, to the echoing boom of cannon, New Brunswick, Nova Scotia and the Province of Canada were proclaimed the Dominion of Canada. Its permanent capital was now Ottawa. John A. Macdonald was its first Prime Minister. Later Governor General Monck gave out honours to those who had worked so hard and so brilliantly to create Canada. That is how John A. became *Sir* John A. Macdonald.

As for Thomas D'Arcy McGee, he was as glad as anyone about the creation of Canada. After all, it was he who had convinced the Irish to support Confederation. But he also harshly criticized the Fenians—he hated secret societies—and for this reason he was unpopular with some Irish Catholics. He was still quite young, but his health was poor and he was always broke. He was said to be the country's greatest orator. On April 6th, 1868, in his last speech in the House of Commons, he defended the idea of Confederation and said that time was an important factor in making it work. He spoke "not as the representative of any race, or of any province, but as thoroughly and emphatically a Canadian".

Among the visitors watching from the gallery was an Irishman by the name Patrick James Whelan. About an hour past midnight McGee left the House, lit a cigar and walked to Mrs. Trotter's boarding house on Spark's Street where he stayed while in Ottawa. It would be his birthday in a few days and he could hardly wait to get home to Montreal and celebrate with his wife and family. He put his key in the lock, started to turn it, and was shot in the head. He died instantly.

Patrick James Whelan was arrested the next day. He was tried and found guilty, though he said he was innocent, and it was never proved that he was a Fenian terrorist. A crowd of five thousand watched him hanged—the last public hanging in Canada. McGee's funeral, on what would have been his forty-third birthday, was the largest that Montreal had ever seen.

XXV
Dominion

…he 1860's consisted of four provinces. In … Montreal was already a big city, with the contrasts between rich and poor that big cities always seem to have.

On the south slope of Mount Royal, in what was called the Square Mile, lived the mostly English-speaking rich families who controlled two thirds of the country's wealth. They had made their money from furs, beer, sugar, flour, shipping. Their names are still familiar today—names like McGill, Molson, Redpath, Ogilvie. The very richest among them was the shipping magnate Hugh Allen who built a big house called Ravenscrag. From the bell tower of his house he could look through a telescope down at the harbour to watch his ships being unloaded.

Many of these men were Scots Presbyterians who had come to the new land with nothing, worked hard, made fortunes, and built houses that looked like castles in a child's dream. They loved being millionaires and they liked to entertain royalty.

In 1860 the Prince of Wales came to visit. In his honour a ball was given for 3,000 guests in a ballroom more than three hundred feet long. The menu for dinner, printed on pink silk, listed sixty dishes including lobster mayonnaise, oysters in aspic, pâté de foie gras, beef, mutton, duck, salmon. Fountains gushed champagne. The prince, popular, young and slim as he then was, stayed and danced until 4:30 in the morning.

On another occasion the prince officially opened the bridge named for his mother, the Victoria railway bridge. It spanned the St. Lawrence and joined Montreal with the United States via the Grand Trunk Railway. It had taken 3,000 men seven years to build it. After the opening the Prince and invited guests went to the Grand Trunk workshops, in the heart of the working class district, to have lunch with the men who had built the bridge. The Prince of Wales spoke to the workers, saying that they could take pride in the fact that the bridge's engineer had come from the working class. He told them that such success was open to anyone who combined talent with hard work. "All cannot claim the prize," he said, "but all may strive for it".

Some years later the Queen's youngest son, Prince Arthur, was posted to Montreal as a subaltern with the Rifle Brigade. He too was entertained, in the summer by Hugh Allen on his yacht, and in the winter at a fancy-dress skating carnival at the Victoria Rink. An observer described it as one of the most beautiful sights he ever beheld. We may still get an impression of this beautifully lit night time scene from a composite photograph by William Notman, a Scot who came to Montreal and became the city's number one photographer. Thanks to him we know today what many people and places looked like then.

Lower down the slope nearer the river lived the working class families—poor and mostly French-speaking. Many of them were Irish immigrants who had come in order to escape the famine in Ireland. Even more of them were French "Canadiens" who had left the land to find work in the city's new industries. In these times when people were too poor to support large families and disease was everywhere, many babies were abandoned. The people who looked after these foundlings were the Grey Nuns. In one year, the year of Confederation, the nuns took in 662 infants, most of whom had died by the end of the year.

One of the nuns who looked after these children was Sister Jane Slocombe. She herself had been an orphan, had survived one earlier cholera epidemic, and quite quickly rose to the top job in the order. (Many older nuns who were helping the sick caught the disease themselves and died at an appalling rate.)

At the Collège de Montréal supervised by the Grey Nuns, one of Sister Slocombe's charges was a Métis named Louis Riel. He had been chosen by Bishop Taché in St. Boniface, in Rupert's Land, as one of four Métis candidates for the priesthood. At first Riel studied hard, though even then he was rather moody. His teachers and others in authority at the college were already thinking he would not make a good priest – he was too unpredictable and unstable. He entertained his classmates with tales of the "exotic" West, of pemmican and tomahawks, of raging prairie grass fires, of fearless hunters and wild horses. While at the college, in 1864, Riel heard the bad news that his father had died. Jean-Louis Riel had been the leader and spokesman for almost six thousand French Métis who lived on the prairie. From here on Louis Riel began to lose interest in becoming a priest and he became even moodier. As he became more and more unhappy and peculiar his friends began to shy away from him.

Sister Slocombe was worried about him: "Louis is still in Montreal", she wrote. "This young man is incomprehensible and behaves most suspiciously. I fear the poor child does not have a good head on his shoulders. He needs someone to guide him.....but here he is on his own and none of his former friends have confidence on him. I fear it will all end badly."

Before graduating Riel left the college and worked as a law clerk so he could send money home to his family in Red River. He was the oldest of eleven children and his father had left no money. He then went to Chicago and St. Paul for a couple of years, then returned to Red River in the summer of 1868—just in time for a plague of grasshoppers. "They penetrated into the parlours and kitchens, bedchambers and bedding, pots, pans, kettles, ovens, boots and coat pockets," it was reported. "One scarcely dared to open one's mouth. On the river they floated like scum or were piled two feet on the banks where they rotted and stank...." They ate the crops, ruined the harvest, and threatened the settlement with famine.

But even worse was to come. A whole way of life was about to change forever, with the sale of Rupert's Land.

The Prince of Wales with entourage in Montreal, 1860

A composite photo of a skating party by William Notman

XXXVI
The Red River Rebellion

On March 20th, 1869, the Hudson Bay Company agreed to sell Rupert's Land to the Government of Canada for 1.5 million dollars. The Americans were eager to buy it – for more money – but the British government would not allow it. The land, including mineral rights, amounted to roughly one quarter of the North American continent, about 5 million square miles. It included parts of northern Quebec, northern Ontario, all of Manitoba, most of the prairies, and parts of what is now Nunavut.

Some Canadians felt an emotional attachment to this land and regarded it as their birthright. Some Americans (they had just bought Alaska from the Russians) felt the same. What was certain, and not so romantic, was expressed in Prime Minister John A. Macdonald's words: "I would be quite willing to leave that whole country a wilderness for the next half century, but I fear that if Englishmen do not go there, Yankees will".

Sadly, no arrangements were made for the people already living there. The sale of Rupert's Land meant the end of the fur trade in the south and the beginning of settlement. Indian services were transferred from the Hudson Bay Company to government-run missions, and the HBC would now do business with settlers, not fur traders. This left the Métis and their way of life hanging in between. Macdonald was sympathetic. As he said to Cartier, "No explanation it appears has been made of the arrangement by which the country is to be handed over. All these poor people know is that Canada has bought the country....and that they are handed over like a flock of sheep to us."

In October of 1869 a survey party was sent by Macdonald to Red River with a view to mapping out the land. This immediately presented a big problem. The British method was to divide land into square sections. This was at odds with the old French method used in Quebec, and still used by Metis farmers, whereby the land was in long strips fronting on a river, with the church at the centre. This created a sense of community not possible with a square survey.

The surveyors turned their attention to the property of André Nault, a Métis farmer. Nault nervously called his cousin, Louis Riel, who arrived, confronted the surveyors and demanded that they stop. The surveyors backed off and went away. This was the beginning of what would become known as the Red River Rebellion. Overnight, Riel became a hero and leader, especially to the 6,000 French-speaking Métis.

The 4,000 English-speaking Métis weren't so sure. They worried that Riel was too hot-headed and spoiling for a fight. Macdonald knew it wouldn't be easy dealing with these "wild" people of the west. He also knew that not everyone would agree with Canada's right to claim all that land. So he proceeded with caution. He sent out William MacDougall as the first Canadian lieutenant-governor of the North West Territories.

Riel responded by sending a group of his men from the National Committee of the Métis to turn MacDougall and his party away at the border. Meanwhile Riel himself rode to the area headquarters at Fort Garry with a group of 120 men, and seized the fort from the elderly, sick governor of Rupert's Land. "Most of us are half breeds," he said. "We all have rights. We claim no half rights....but all the rights we are entitled to. Those rights will be set out by our representatives and what is more, we will get them." He then drew up a list of rights which declared, in short, that the Métis would accept union with Canada as long as they could keep their property, their Catholic religion, and their French language.

The Grey Nuns at their mission in Red River were sympathetic to Riel's cause. But back in Montreal Sister Jane Slocombe was worried that they might get tangled up in politics: "I know I do not need to tell you to be very watchful so that no indiscretions are committed, spoken or written. Our sisters must remain silent on all political matters."

There was a further complication: Since the 1860s there had been an influx of settlers from Ontario. Just when the Red River colony was going so well, these newcomers elbowed their way into the community and, with their inflated sense of entitlement, (they called it "manifest destiny"), upset the balance between the HBC, the Scots half-breeds and the Metis. This caused a lot of trouble.

There were rumours that a drugstore owner in Winnipeg named John Christian Schultz was planning an armed resistance to Riel and had put a price on his head. Riel's reaction was to capture 45 of Schultz's followers and put them in the stockade. Then he set up his own provisional government for Red River.

Macdonald tried to soothe Riel's feelings by offering him amnesty, money and employment for Métis leaders, as well as assurances that their land titles would be respected by the Canadian government. Riel agreed to negotiate terms with Ottawa for Red River to enter Confederation. He then released the men he held at Fort Garry.

Schultz's people, however, wouldn't give up. This time they went to Portage la Prairie to gain support from the Scottish people there to overthrow Riel's provisional government. Again Riel captured the lot of them and put them in the Fort Garry stockade.

Among the captives was Thomas Scott, a big, loud Ontario Orangeman who hurled insults at his guards and made threats against Riel. Riel's patience snapped; he overreacted. The Orangeman was tried for "treason", convicted, sentenced to death and executed by firing squad in the courtyard of Fort Garry.

Riel had made a big mistake. Up to now he had seemed not unreasonable. But this was murder. A body of 1200 British troops under the command of Colonel Garnet Wolsely was sent out to Red River to deal with the situation. It took the soldiers three months and forty-one portages, often across muskeg and all the time being eaten by mosquitoes, before they reached Fort Garry. After this heroic journey they entered the fort—only to find it empty except for Riel's hastily abandoned breakfast. Riel was watching them from horseback, a quarter of a mile away.

The soldiers, in a rage of frustration, took it out on local people, especially one of the jurors in Scott's trial who died trying to escape. No arrests were made. Winnipeg and the whole territory were in chaos. There was much bad feeling.

French Canadians, among them Bishop Taché of St. Boniface, believed that the west should be open to them as much as to English Protestants. What happened in Manitoba would be important to show whether or not the government intended to keep this promise.

Yet Ottawa, quietly and behind the scenes, had agreed to most of the conditions in Riel's list of rights. On May 12th, 1870, the Manitoba Act was passed, and Manitoba became Canada's fifth province.

Riel himself became a fugitive from justice; his demand for amnesty was not granted. He lived in exile in the United States for a time, then returned to Canada, was twice elected to a Federal seat in the Manitoba riding of Provencher, and was twice expelled from the House in Ottawa—because he was still wanted for murder. After that he returned, for the time being, to exile.

The Execution of Thomas Scott

Thomas Scott

XXXVII
British Columbia

In the meantime, what had been happening on the West Coast?

It was almost a century since Captain Cook's last voyage. In that time the land west of the Rockies had been carrying on all by itself, almost completely cut off from the rest of the Northwest.

After Captain Cook's adventures in the late 1700's, (as well as some disagreements with the Spanish over trading rights with the natives), Captain George Vancouver returned and very carefully mapped the coast all the way from Oregon to Alaska. It took him three years.

At the same time, from the east, came Alexander Mackenzie, David Thompson and Simon Fraser, seeking to open up the interior for the fur trade. The Hudson Bay company controlled the western fur trade, even including the present-day states of Washington and Oregon. As American settlers moved west into this territory there was a good deal of bickering about who had the authority there—the United States or the HBC.

In 1846 it was decided by treaty that the southern boundary of British territory would run along the 49th parallel, except for Vancouver Island. The HBC's new headquarters was in Fort Victoria. A few years later Vancouver Island became a colony. James Douglas, an official of the Hudson Bay Company, was its first governor. By the middle of the 19th century the only white settlements in what was to become British Columbia were fur trading posts on the coasts, such as Victoria, Nanaimo and Fort Langley, and in the interior: Kamloops, Fort George and Fort St. James. Life was relatively quiet and uneventful.

Then suddenly—there was gold.

In 1857 someone discovered gold in the lower Fraser River, and people started pouring in from everywhere, all rushing to seek their fortunes.

Many were Californians who had just been having a gold rush there, had exhausted their luck, and thought they would try further north. (A "mining frontier" ran all the way up the continent, starting in California in 1849 and later ending in the Klondike in 1898). The boomtown of Barkerville sprang up almost overnight to the west of the Cariboo Mountains and became (for a while) the largest settlement in western Canada.

To keep law and order amid all this pandemonium the British government established another colony on the mainland and called it British Columbia. James Douglas was the governor of it as well. The capital was New Westminster. From this spot on the Fraser, river traffic could be controlled. In the 1860's, in order to move supplies to the settlements in the interior, they built the amazing Cariboo Road, carved into the rock of the canyon walls high above the churning, roaring waters of the Fraser River.

During this rush for gold, prospectors found it difficult to travel in the B.C. interior. They needed more pack animals. But instead of using ponies or mules, someone had the bright idea of bringing camels from the Middle East. The camels were unsuited to the mountains, however. They were soon let loose, and for a while there was a wild camel population in the B.C. interior.

Eventually the gold petered out and people began to leave. To reduce costs the British government made the two colonies into one, with New Westminster as its capital. But this did not sit well with people in the original capital. After two years of protests the capital was moved back again to Victoria.

In March of 1867, about the same time as the signing of Confederation in the east, the United States had bought Alaska. At this point B.C. felt *really* isolated, hemmed in by Americans both to the north and to the south, and by the Rockies to the east. Their population was small, less than 40,000, and three quarters of those were natives. The United States government had even tried to get B.C. for themselves, but the British government had refused.

It became clear that the best alternative to being swallowed up by the United States was to join Confederation. Among those arguing for this course of action was someone who called himself by the unlikely name of Amor de Cosmos. His real name was William Smith and he had come from Nova Scotia, founded a newspaper called the "British Colonist", and got himself elected to the Vancouver Island assembly where he became leader of the opposition. He liked to parade about town with a walking stick, which he would use as a weapon whenever he got into a fight.

The British government now wanted British Columbia to join Canada as soon as possible. In 1870 a delegation from B.C. went to Ottawa to discuss terms with Cartier. They timidly suggested that perhaps a wagon road might be built from Lake Superior to the Pacific—not very expensive (but not very practical either). To their great surprise Cartier offered them a railway instead. Construction would begin within two years and be completed in ten. Not only that, but Cartier also agreed to take over the colony's debt and pay them an annual subsidy besides.

In 1871 British Columbia entered Confederation, becoming the sixth province to join the Dominion. The next year Amor de Cosmos became premier—the first of that province's rather unusual leaders, but not the last.

[Two years later, in 1873, Prince Edward Island accepted a similar offer of subsidies from the government in Ottawa and became Province Number Seven.]

Amor di Cosmos

The Cariboo Road above the Fraser River

Port of Vancouver, 1899

Cariboo Camel

XXXVIII
Migrations

So—a railway had been promised. But first there were many hurdles to be got over, and not everything went according to plan.

For one thing, the railway was not popular with people in Ontario. Then the project, and the government, were brought down by what became known as the Pacific Scandal. It seems Hugh Allen had raised the money to build the railway by selling shares to Americans, without telling Macdonald. Macdonald, furious with Allen, was forced to resign.

He was succeeded by a Liberal, Alexander Mackenzie, (*another* Alexander Mackenzie), who had very different views from Macdonald. He was a stonemason from Sarnia, Ontario, a stubborn man with little education, whose main aim was to save money. This meant stopping the railway building. His plans, however, were spoiled by the onset of an economic depression that overtook Europe and North America—the worst of the 19th century. Factories closed, jobs were lost, wages were lowered and children put to work. Many faced starvation or nearly froze because the price of fuel was beyond them. There was much despair and abuse of alcohol; the Women's Christian Temperance Union came into being in Ontario, to fight the evils of drink.

Many jobless people left the cities and went to the United States, or else headed west where there was fresh air and free land to be had. Over the next twenty years land speculators would turn the "wild west" into real estate, and settlers would begin to come from Ontario, Europe and Great Britain. And a railway *would* be built, eventually, but not quite on schedule.

Across the river from Winnipeg lay St. Boniface, the Métis settlement where Bishop Taché was in charge of the largest Catholic church in the North-West. Here the way of life was threatened. The Manitoba

Act guaranteed French religion and schools, as Riel had insisted, but even so, waves of English-speaking settlers were upsetting the Métis, stirring up religious and racial trouble with their bad manners and insults. A Métis by the name of Louis Goulet wrote: "Newcomers, especially the ones from Ontario, were eagerly..... banding together to fan the flames of discord between different groups in the Red River Settlement. These émigrés from Ontario, all of them Orangemen, looked as if their one dream in life was to make war on the Hudson Bay Company, the Catholic Church, and anyone who spoke French." Certainly it looked as though they would soon outnumber the French and have more influence in Ottawa if something were not done.

Father Albert Lacombe, the parish priest at St. Mary's in Winnipeg, had to agree. Although he had already been living in the west for twenty years and had braved blizzards, prairie grass fires and Cree warriors, he saw Orangemen as a greater danger. He thought the best way to preserve French life and language was to get Quebecers, including those who had gone to the States, to move to Manitoba.

Another person besides Father Lacombe who was busy recruiting Frenchmen in the factories of New England in the 1870's, was Louis Riel. Still living in exile, he went about giving political speeches, seeking help for the Métis cause. Little by little his political speeches began to develop a religious tone. He began to tell his French-Canadian audiences that God was speaking directly to him. "When I speak to you," he said, "it is the voice of God that sounds.....I am the happy telephone who transmits the songs and messages of heaven". He told a parish priest in Massachusetts that he was a prophet of God. The priest thought Riel was having delusions and asked for help. Early in 1876 Riel was diagnosed with megalomania and quietly removed, first to Beauport and then to Long Pointe, both insane asylums in Quebec, where he spent two years. His identity was kept secret to protect him from Canadian bounty hunters; he was, after all, still wanted in Ontario for murder.

Meanwhile Canadian voters, tired of Alexander Mackenzie's penny-pinching ways, had returned John A. Macdonald to office as Prime Minister. He at once set about resuming construction of the C.P.R., and advertising for immigrants in central Canada, England, Scotland and Europe. Many of the posters and pamphlets, meant to lure farmers to land along where the railroad would pass, were more romantic then strictly truthful. They promised a Utopia where people could make a new start in a new society. The government was offering 160 acres for a mere $10 deposit, and people began to arrive in growing numbers—first in a trickle, then in a flood.

But they soon found that the reality was somewhat different from the posters. Some of these pioneers travelled huge distances by horse and cart along crude tracks, for example from Winnipeg to Prince Albert in what is now Saskatchewan. They tell of struggling through gumbo mud and thick clouds of mosquitoes. One young bride was so crazed by the mosquitoes that she shot herself. Another family built and finished a cabin just before Christmas in minus 50 degree weather. It was so cold that it made the horses' noses bleed. Some English settlers went by CPR to Grenfell, Saskatchewan, or further on to Regina, the husband first building a small wooden box of a house, the wife following on later from Winnipeg. One can imagine the sight that met her eyes, and what she must have thought when she realized that the next few years would be lived in isolation, in what looked to her like a chicken coop. Other immigrants just arriving in Winnipeg found a rough place, scarcely a city, where in the summer, if you stepped off the wooden sidewalks, you would sink up to your knees in gluey mud. Very few of the early settlers' experiences were what they had expected

Another thing the immigration pamphlets had not mentioned about the prairies: the people already there, the natives. All these changes were bound to disrupt the Indians' way of life. As one Cree chief later said, "The iron road has frightened the game away and the talking wire stretches from sunrise to sunset." The Plains Indians also faced the devastations of whiskey and disease, as well as the loss of the buffalo herds. Never before had they been so in need of a guide and leader.

Wagons Alberta bound

A sod house

XXXIX
The Great Plains
Part 1

Crowfoot was born into the Blood tribe about 1830 in the Belly River country near present-day Lethbridge, Alberta. When Crowfoot was two his father had been killed and his mother remarried a warrior of the Blackfoot tribe. By the time he was twenty he had fought nearly twenty battles, the first when he was fourteen, mostly against the Plains Cree. He was wounded six times, once by a bullet that was never removed. At twenty he was given his name, "Crow Indians' Big Foot", after a daring raid on a Crow camp. Eventually he became chief of the Blackfoot, the most powerful chief on the prairies. Unlike most of his race he did not share in all native spiritual beliefs. All his life, for whatever reason, he wore an owl's skull tied into his long black hair. His face was fine-boned, calm—a beautiful face, that of a thinker, perhaps a poet. He was intelligent, short-tempered and brave.

Crowfoot was chief during a time of sudden change like never before on the prairies—a time of whiskey traders, smallpox outbreaks, the end of the buffalo herds and the beginning of settlement. All this happened within a mere ten years, in the 1870s. Father Lacombe probably did as much as any single person could to prepare the way for this great change. During a long career in the west he worked among the Cree and the Blackfoot, spoke both their languages (he had a Métis grandmother), and worked toward peace among the tribes. He supervised the building of the first bridge in Alberta and started the first school in the territory, at Fort Edmonton. The Blackfoot called him "The Man of Good Heart". (When Lacombe died in 1916 both Blackfoot and Cree claimed his body, so they compromised: his body was buried in Cree country, at St. Albert, and his heart went to Midnapore, south of Calgary, in Blackfoot country).

When the early missionaries first came to the prairies it was during a time of constant warfare, Blackfoot against Cree. Lacombe met Crowfoot for the first time while the Blackfoot were wintering on the Battle River, and Lacombe was just starting on his first mission. It nearly killed him.

One day he was trying to convert Crowfoot to Christianity, when the Blackfoot camp was attacked by the Plains Cree—800 of them against only 80 Blackfoot. In the midst of whining bullets, musket fire, shrieks, groans, war whoops, dogs barking, warriors shouting—Father Lacombe tried to intervene. He stood between the two armies, arms raised, his cassock black against the snow, trying to stop the fighting with words of peace. A bullet whizzed by, grazing his forehead, and he fell down unconscious. Two Blackfoot warriors dragged him back to safety.

This was one of the last big battles between the Blackfoot and the Cree; the war between them ended in 1869. Their next big battle was with alcohol.

In the 1870's traders came from Fort Benton, Montana, up the Whoop-Up Trail, to trading posts in southern Alberta and on into Blackfoot territory, near where the Bow and Elbow rivers meet. Like the Hudson Bay Company before them, they traded rifles, blankets, iron pots, in exchange for furs and other trade goods. But unlike the HBC they also offered "whiskey".

They called it Whoop-Up Bug Juice and it was made, cheaply, of distilled alcohol mixed with chewing tobacco, soap, molasses, red pepper and red ink. It was pure poison. In just three years it came close to destroying the Plains Indians, doing more damage than a hundred years of tribal warfare. Crowfoot described its effects:

"The whiskey brought among us by the traders is fast killing us off and we are powerless before this evil. We are unable to resist the temptation to drink...the white man's water. Our horses, buffalo robes....go for whiskey. A large number of our people have killed one another and perished under the influence."

A Cree camp

Buffalo scratcher

Col. Macleod

NWMP comissioner French and colleagues

At Fort Macleod

Father Lacombe

XL
The Great Plains
Part 2

In 1874 the North West Mounted Police began their march west. The year before, American hunters had "massacred" 20 Assiniboines in the Cypress Hills in what is now southeastern Alberta and southwestern Saskatchewan. This was the final blow which had helped to convince the powers in Ottawa that a police force was needed in the west. For some time the Canadian government had been anxious that Indian lands should not be occupied by force and bloody warfare, as was the case in the United States. Now was the time to start sending in the peace keepers.

The officer corps of the NWMP was made up mainly of Canadians, drawn initially from the ranks of the Canadian Militia (later from the new Royal Military College) and some United Empire Loyalists. A large minority came from the British Army. All were united by a determination to uphold "British" law.

The ranks of the NWMP consisted mainly of farm boys and store clerks from Ontario, Quebec and the Maritimes, who signed up in exchange for a horse, a scarlet uniform and 75 cents a day (and probably for the adventure). Over thirty of them changed their minds and disappeared before the march had even begun. The rest endured three months of little food, little water, dying horses, and lots and lots of mosquitoes. In October of 1874, 251 men and 24 officers arrived at the Oldman River in southern Alberta where they built a fort (later named after the commissioner, Colonel Macleod) and proceeded to stop the whiskey trade. They very quickly brought law and order to the territory, with very little violence and very few men. This impressed the Plains chiefs. One Cree chief said:

"The Great Queen Mother, hearing of the sorrows of her children, sent out the Red Coats. Though these were only of a number you could count on your fingers and toes, yet the cutthroats and criminals who recognized no authority but their guns, who killed each other on the slightest pretence and murdered Indians without fear of reprisal, immediately abandoned their forts, strong as they were, and fled back to their own side of the line. I ask you why those few men could put to flight those bad men who for years have defied the whole of the southern Indian nations?....Let me tell you why these things were so. It was the power that stands behind those few Red Coats that those men feared, and wasted no time in getting out when they could..."

The whiskey trade was stopped, but still the buffalo were disappearing. Thc buffalo meant everything to the Plains Indians: their food, their clothing and their shelter. Once there had been 50 million of them on the Great Plains of North America, herds so vast that it took several days to pass them on horseback. But by the end of the decade, tens of millions had been slaughtered for "sport" or commercial gain. In the United States they were nearly extinct, thanks to the government's military policy: get rid of the buffalo and free the land for cattle ranching. Buffalo hunters in the U.S. burned the grasslands at the Canadian border to prevent what animals remained from escaping to the north.

As the railway advanced steadily westward across the prairies the Canadian government smoothed the way by making treaties with the Indians whose land it would cross. On August 15th, 1876, two thousand natives made camp on the plains outside Fort Carlton on the North Saskatchewan River. They were about to meet with the treaty commissioner, Alexander Morris, and sign the largest land treaty in the history of North America. The deal involved the transfer of over 200 thousand square miles, most of the prairie provinces. In exchange, the Dominion government took on the responsibility for the "protection and well-being " of the treaty Indians, including missionary education (which later became compulsory), housing, medicine and help in times of disease or famine, as well as help in learning to farm, and gifts of seeds, ploughs and harrows to get them started. Each native family would receive one square mile of land to farm, in addition to their old hunting and fishing rights. The following year, in 1877, the last of this first group of "numbered treaties", Treaty #7, was signed at Blackfoot Crossing on the reserve east of present-day Calgary.

Most of the Plains chiefs signed the treaty, at least symbolically. None actually signed his name or even marked an X; they simply touched the pen that someone else had used to sign their names for them. Thus matters were settled peacefully, at least for the time being.

Some natives were less than thrilled with the "bounteous presents from the Great Mother", notably the Cree chiefs Poundmaker and Big Bear. An observer watched Big Bear "every day riding round the camp on an Indian pony, haughty and defiant, his face and body adorned with war paint, and his long black hair decorated with eagle feathers while he carried a gaudy parasol over his head.

But most natives realized their old world was gone, and if they were to survive, they were in no position to choose. Crowfoot, speaking in 1877, said it best: "We all see the day is coming when the buffalo will all be killed, and we shall have nothing more to live on....then you will come into our camp and see the poor Blackfoot starving. I know that the heart of the white soldier will be sorry for us and they will tell the Great Mother who will not let her children starve. We are getting shut in. The Crees are coming into our country from the north, and the white men from the south and east, and they are all destroying our means of living....we plainly see these days coming..."

It was for this reason, and in keeping with their responsibilities according to the treaty, that the Dominion Government instituted what would through the next century cause so much trouble – the residential schools. They began with the best of intentions. The buffalo were gone and the Indians needed to learn how to farm, amongst other things. Indeed, in the 1870s these schools were seen as the only hope; ironically, many in authority expressed the belief that, lacking such education, the Native people would "disappear from the face of the earth". At first, chiefs and other parents sent their sons to school so they would learn to survive and become leaders in a changed world.

But very soon things started to go bad. Although attendance was not strictly speaking compulory until 1920, it was "encouraged" by the withholding of treaty money and rations in the event of non-compliance. Families became divided, children from parents. The pass system, meant as a way of keeping peace and order by separating Indians from settlers, only made things worse. As time wore on there were more abuses, by some

Indian agents and school authorities, many of which amounted to criminal behaviour. All this was ignored by the Dominion government, much too far away in Ottawa. It seems that the eventual failure of the residential schools was not through intent, but through ignorance and neglect. The Dominion government had promised to look after the Indians' well-being; instead they were causing misery. They were *not* keeping their promise.

Meanwhile, Father Lacombe looked out across the prairies at the road that was rapidly cutting its way through his beloved Indians' ancient homeland, bringing with it towns and farms and settlers; and he worried about the future.

Crowfoot

Fort Whoop-Up

XLI
Moving West

The building of the transcontinental railway resumed in 1878, after the "Pacific Scandal" had blown over and Macdonald was again Prime Minister. But it was still a troubled enterprise, and by now the promised deadline was only three years away. Some of it had already been built by Hugh Allen and other contractors but the biggest and hardest parts—across the prairies and through the Rockies—had yet to be done.

A new railway syndicate was formed by George Stephen, president of the Bank of Montreal. Besides several other rich and influential men, the syndicate included a silent partner, Donald Smith. "Silent" meant that, although he had money and influence, his name was not put on the government contract. The other partners in the syndicate feared that his very name would upset Macdonald, who had loathed Smith ever since the "Pacific Scandal" when Smith had loudly and publicly complained about corruption in the Conservative party. The government guaranteed the syndicate a $25 million loan and granted it title to 25 million acres of prairie real estate.

The government loan dwindled fast, however—as with many large projects the original cost estimates turned out to be much too low, and not much new money was coming in. In order to cut costs the syndicate rejected the route mapped out by Sandford Fleming, the C.P.R. chief engineer. This route was intended to go north west from Red River through Saskatoon, Edmonton, and through the Rockies by the Yellowhead Pass. Instead the syndicate decided it would be cheaper to take a southern route, besides cutting off competition from American lines (They ordered the CPR to be built through Calgary toward the Rockies without any idea of whether they could find a pass. By great good luck, the CPR surveyor

Rogers happened to see eagles soaring in the distance and knew there must be a pass – Eagle Pass!).

Then in 1882, just when the deadline was already a year past and prospects were looking bleak, in strode the man who was to take over the construction contract, William Cornelius Van Horne. Larger than life, devil-may-care: "I eat all I can, drink all I can, I smoke all I can, and I don't give a damn for anything", he said. He promised to build 500 miles of track in one year—and kept his promise. Sometimes he performed hard physical labour on the line himself, eating five big meals a day, drinking all night and working from the crack of dawn again next day. In this manner the railway roared ahead like a prairie grass fire.

Hopes were now high for some settlements across the west. When the people of Winnipeg learned that the railway would pass through their city, they went mad with excitement. Everyone seemed to be selling real estate (some of it existing only on paper); there was a building boom, diamonds and champagne were everywhere in evidence, scores of telephones were installed, fortunes were made (also mostly on paper), and the population doubled. The city was ablaze with excitement. But after a year and a half the blaze burnt itself out, the river flooded and washed out the bridges as Sandford Fleming had predicted, and the land speculators moved on.

Edmonton also experienced a boom, briefly, until the route was changed to go through Calgary instead. All along the proposed route westward from Winnipeg settlements of Ontarians and British remittance men sprang up, some hoping to recreate England on the prairies. There were cricket, fox-hunting, tennis parties. Alice Hewett, one of the early settlers at Cannington Manor south of present-day Moosomin, Saskatchewan, later described the life:

"Once upon a time there was magic in the name of Cannington Manor....In those days it was a gallant adventure upon which the early settlers set out. The railway had come no nearer than Brandon; reports were what they had to go upon...of a land where milk and honey could be made to flow. So they set out from England and Scotland and ...Ontario, and found their way to the prairie east of the Moose Mountains......Tea was served on Tennis Courts by the ladies...Intermingling with their pretty summer frocks could be seen young men in flannels wearing the blazers and colours of all the best known English and Scottish public schools.....Then back, usually in a buckboard, home to dress for dinner, to dine with friends or attend ....a dance, card party, midnight frolic, drive or ride to the lake."

But the railway never did come near enough, and after a time the town disappeared. Instead, British tradition moved farther west, into the foothills of the Rockies.

Poster luring immigrants west

Log cabin - Calgary, 1885

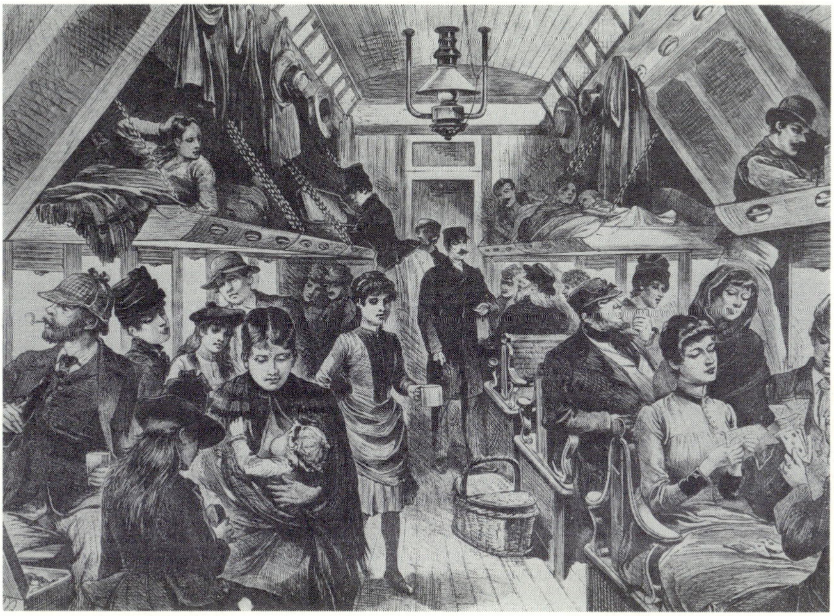

Immigrant train going west

Winnipeg in 1870

Winnipeg's main street, 1880s

XLII
Cowboys and Indians

Just about the time when Macdonald and the railway-building were starting up again, Crowfoot and the Blackfoot had decided to go south across the border in search of buffalo. The Indian commissioner did not discourage them, for he thought that not having to feed the natives would save the Canadian government money. But by the following year the buffalo were nearly all gone and the U.S. army loomed on the horizon. Crowfoot wrote to the Indian commissioner and asked if the Great Mother would feed them, as promised by treaty. The commissioner replied that they should continue after the buffalo. The few remaining herds then huddled together in central Montana where he Blackfoot, Sioux and Cree joined in the last great hunt. After that Crowfoot and Big Bear camped near Fort Carrol, Montana.

Not far away, living quietly with his family and teaching school, was Louis Riel. He had been released a couple of years before from the Quebec insane asylum, and now began talking to Big Bear and stirring up feeling against the government. "Riel wanted me to raise all the men I could but I wouldn't", Big Bear said later. "Many wanted to fight in 1879 but I stopped them." Still, the seeds of rebellion had been planted.

In the meantime Crowfoot was forced to deal again with the whiskey traders. Soon the Blackfoot were in a sorrier state than ever, having sold off everything they owned for whiskey, and dying of measles, starvation and exposure in the cold winter. In the late summer of 1881 they started out for home, a 380 mile trek northward to Fort Walsh in the Cypress Hills. It took them six weeks.

A North West Mounted Police doctor touring their encampments reported that they were "literally in a starving condition." "The disappearance of the buffalo ," he wrote, "has left them not only without food, but also without robes, moccasins and adequate tents or 'tipis' to shield them from... the impending winter...It would be difficult to exaggerate their extreme wretchedness and need...for some prompt and sufficient provision being made for them by the government."

The deputy superintendent of Indian affairs, knowing the government in these hard economic times was looking for ways to cut back on spending, toured the western reserves and gave his opinion that the government was already spending too much, and should rather cut back on native rations. Local Indian agents and the NWMP were horrified and argued against such a policy; whereupon the superintendent wrote to the government suggesting that agents in the field should be disregarded, and the decision-making power should all be in Ottawa. After that the natives were put on half rations, a policy referred to by some as "feed one day, starve the next".

The meat doled out in these rations came from ranches in the foothills of the Rockies where the grazing lands, now free of buffalo, were just right for cattle. The first of these large operations, the Cochrane Ranch Company, was started by Matthew Cochrane, a Tory senator from Quebec. The government allowed land to be leased for 1 cent an acre. Cochrane leased altogether 360,000 acres (over 560 square miles), mostly west and south of Calgary. In 1881, at the same time as Crowfoot and his band were returning north across the border, the first cattle were brought into Alberta. Over 9,000 head of Black Angus and Shorthorn were driven up through Montana by American cowhands. Canadians took over at the border and drove them further north, moving about 15 miles a day until they reached the Bow River, then forded it.

The Cochrane Ranch company was run by people in the east, through Cochrane and his business partners. Everything was fine that first mild winter when the cattle could graze. But the Montrealers were far away and probably didn't know much about Alberta or ranching. Assuming that the next winter would be like the first, they failed to put up any winter feed for the cattle. During the winter of 1882 the temperature dropped to 35 degrees below zero and the snow was so deep that the animals couldn't get to the grass underneath. Most of them starved. When spring came and snow melted the land was strewn with thousands of dead cattle.

After this initial disaster the ranchers learned from their mistakes and the ranching industry began to run smoothly. In time a new society grew up, one with its own unique flavour—both proudly agrarian and oddly cosmopolitan—lasting well into the 20th century.

Most of the earliest ranches were owned by investors in the east or in Britain who sent out their sons to run operations for them. Through them the British tradition that had failed to take root at Cannington Manor began to flourish in southern Alberta. There were formal balls, polo and cricket, and coyote-hunting (instead of fox-hunting). Their ranches supplied meat to the NWMP and the natives on reserves.

But not enough of it got to the natives. During the winter of 1883-84 there was threat of starvation. During this period the Mounties were feeding many Cree and Blackfoot from their own supplies. The buffalo were gone and the government was forced to provide aid to the Plains tribes, but they didn't want native groups to become dependent on handouts. For several years the government tried to get them to move onto the reserves where they would be given food in exchange for work, but many didn't want to—being "fenced in" was alien to their nature. Poundmaker spoke about the need for more teachers to educate their children, for more land, and for more farm implements so they could work their land. Poundmaker and Big Bear really wanted to hold out and continue the old ways for as long as possible, but they feared that without help future generations would starve.

Problems were plaguing white settlers as well. Many needed money to buy farm equipment, but to get a loan from the bank they needed to have title to their land—which many didn't have. Ottawa didn't help. The protective tariffs which were good for manufacturers in the east were anything but good for settlers in the west. Adding to their woes was the high price of shipping grain to the east.

William Jackson, a University of Toronto philosophy student living in Prince Albert, took action. He organized the Settlers' Union, a first move toward getting provincial legislatures for the North West Territories. Jackson went to both Métis and British settlers with his plans to revolt against the government. For a time westerners were united in purpose; but soon their differences made them split up again into white settlers, Métis and natives.

Big Bear organized a meeting of more than 2000 Crees on Poundmaker's reserve, supposedly for a traditional Thirst Dance. The aim was political unity, not military—he believed actual war would be a disaster.

On one occasion the police superintendent tried to arrest a native for assaulting a farm instructor over a sack of flour. The Mounties suddenly found themselves surrounded by Cree warriors. The chiefs did all they could to make the man give up quietly. Both sides feared that one shot fired would be the signal for a Native uprising. The episode ended without violence, but it was clear to the government that things had been badly mismanaged, and that they would have to feed the natives or suffer the consequences. It was also clear that Big Bear had failed to unite the bands.

The government brought Crowfoot, viewed as the most powerful Plains chief, east to Winnipeg for a visit. They hoped to impress him with the white man's military strength and the power of his civilization. They showed him the Stony Mountain Penitentiary, the armoury with its large store of weapons, and buildings and streets lit by electric lights. Crowfoot was certainly impressed by the electric lights.

He asked how many days a week the people of Winnipeg had food.

Fort Calgary

Fort Macleod - Church of the Holy Cross

XLIII
The Riel Rebellion
Part 1

The time was ripe. In 1884, into the midst of all this misery, anger, confusion and disillusionment with the government, Louis Riel returned, like the prophet that he claimed to be. Of course the Métis were already thinking about rebellion as the only way to get the government in Ottawa to listen to them. Macdonald warned that Riel was someone to keep an eye on.

His suspicions were justified. Riel and the head of the settlers' union formed an alliance, and Riel again asked the support of the Blackfoot and the Cree, through a meeting with Chief Big Bear. Macdonald asked bishop Grandin to go to Batoche and find out just what Riel had in mind.

Grandin's report was alarming: "The Métis spoke to me of Riel with extraordinary enthusiasm. For them he was a saint; I would say rather a kind of God." Apparently Riel thought the same of himself. In a letter to Bishop Taché, Grandin wrote that "Riel is a dangerous man who could cause real trouble."

Meanwhile the Saskatchewan settlers and Métis sent a petition to the government asking for four things: deeds (title) to their land; tariff reductions; control of natural resources; and the right to vote for elected representatives. Then they waited through a long winter for a reply. In February came a pale response from Ottawa suggesting a commission to look into Métis land claims. Riel, increasingly delusional, set up a "provisional government of the Saskatchewan" at Batoche, and preached "battle to the death".

While all this was going on a letter came to Macdonald from George Stephen saying that the CPR was going bankrupt; without more government money the railway building would have to stop. Macdonald now had two problems. He decided to use the threat of rebellion as an excuse to put government money into the railway, as a more practical way of transporting troops quickly to deal with the rebellion. (It had taken Wolsely's men more than three months to get to Red River—hardly quick enough).

On the same day that Stephen's letter arrived, Supt. Leif Crozier was moving in on Batoche with 56 Mounties, 41 Prince Albert Volunteers and one 7-pound piece of artillery. He hoped to be in time to stop Riel before his force of 1000 or so Métis was joined (as he no doubt imagined) by several more thousands of Plains natives. Nobody wanted the kind of Indian wars that were going on in the American West.

Gabriel Dumont was a Métis buffalo hunter who, as a horseman and a rifleman, was already a legend in his own time. Before he came under Riel's influence he had been a peacemaker who arranged treaties between the Métis and the Blackfoot and helped settle disputes. Now he was Riel's loyal military commander.

One day Dumont's brother Isadore and a Cree native rode out toward Crozier's men who were camped at Duck Lake, intending to stop the Metis from acquiring weapons from the post. Dumont waved a white blanket as a flag of truce. A Mountie interpreter rode out to meet them. Before anyone quite knew what was happening, a misunderstanding involving the Mountie's rifle led Crozier to suspect an ambush—he could see Métis moving about in the bush nearby—and he ordered his men to open fire. Both the Cree and Isadore were killed. But Crozier's men, out in the open with no cover, were immediately shot at by Métis from behind bushes. Crozier had to retreat, with twelve dead, eleven wounded and five horses killed. Only four Métis and one native died at Duck Lake.

Riel, feeling secure in the righteousness of his cause, claimed victory. The settlers' reactions, on the other hand, ranged from fear and dismay to indifference. They supported Riel's cause, but had no desire for an armed battle, and certainly no wish for an Indian uprising. Some were just too busy with their own problems of early frosts and failing crops. And many of them thought Riel was unhinged. After Duck Lake Riel lost the support of most settlers.

In Prince Albert some of the settlers' native employees began wearing war paint and disappearing into the bush headed toward Duck Lake. The people living on the outskirts were advised to go into town. Some men, and most children, thought it all very exciting, especially when the NWMP and the militias began clattering by with their horses and wagons.

At Fort Edmonton settlers left their farms and took refuge inside the fort. When the drums stopped and the natives' tents disappeared overnight from their camp near the fort, the settlers knew it was time to prepare for war.

Macdonald sent Father Lacombe to see what was happening, hoping that he would influence Crowfoot. But Lacombe reported that, in effect, it was too late, and that most Indians were no longer interested in white policy. Militias under the command of General Frederick Middleton were being sent from Halifax, Toronto, Winnipeg and Quebec (though some in Quebec were squeamish about fighting against "Frenchmen like us"). Within two weeks after Duck Lake troops had begun arriving at Winnipeg, and Middleton set out for Batoche.

Riel was in a dangerous position: only about half of the Saskatchewan Métis were behind him now, and the settlers' union no longer supported him at all.

He needed the Indians.

Riel as a child, with his mother

Portrait of Gabriel Dumont

General Middleton's troops riding to Batoche

Louis Riel

Gabriel Dumont with his horse

XLIV
The Riel Rebellion
Part 2

Crowfoot did not want the Blackfoot to go to war. He knew it would only lead to slaughter. He did, however, use his political advantage and the danger of an uprising to get more food for his people. Macdonald responded by ordering that rations be sent, not just to Crowfoot's band, but to "wherever the tomahawks are sharpest", as he put it. Crowfoot then pledged his support to the Prime Minister in a telegram:

"Continued reports and many lies are brought to us and we don't know what to believe, but now that we have seen the Governor and heard him speak, we will shut our ears and only listen to and believe what is told to us by the Governor. Should any Indians come to our reserve and ask us to join them in war, we will send them away".

Riel was now left with only the Cree.

Big Bear did not agree with Riel's actions at Duck Lake, but he had lost control over his warriors, who were hungry and made bold by the Métis victory. From his band's camp near Frog Lake a group of warriors led by Wandering Spirit, their faces painted red, went forth and attacked the settlement. Amid whoops, war cries and shots they looted the store, took prisoners, then killed nine white men, including two priests. After that Big Bear and his band went north to escape the army and avoid joining Riel at Batoche.

There were other skirmishes, including one in which a government farm instructor was shot by some Stoneys for refusing to give them flour, and another next day during which a rancher was killed. Through it all the natives were driven by hunger. It was not clear to anyone whether these native forces would form a reliable army behind Riel.

Nor was it known how reliable the militia from eastern Canada would prove to be. At Fort Qu'Appelle, from where they were to advance on Batoche, General Middleton reviewed his men. He discovered that many of them had never fired a rifle, and some of them had never fired any weapon at all. "This", remarked Middleton, "was not a cheerful outlook after receiving a telegram dwelling on the excellence of the shooting of the half-breeds."

Riel was becoming ever more peculiar, convinced that God was directing his military decisions. He argued with his general, Dumont, who saw the practical advantages of Guerilla warfare and wanted to blow up the railway line, an obviously shrewd, quick and decisive tactic. But Riel wanted something more grand and theatrical. He sent Dunont out to delay Middleton, perhaps hoping that more natives would join them in the meantime. Dumont, with 135 men, waited for Middleton's 800 troops at Fish Creek ravine south of Batoche. Dumont's marksmen, from behind dense cover, easily overcame the eastern recruits, and the day ended with Middleton's fifty-five casualties to Dumont's four.

Riel then sent agents to the Cree led by Poundmaker near Fort Battleford, demanding that they send him forty or fifty men. Poundmaker, like Crowfoot and Big Bear, thought war against white troops was a fool's game, but he, too, found his young warriors hard to control. They were already raiding food stores. Middleton sent Col. W.D. Otter to confront Poundmaker's band in retaliation. Once again the 325 militia men and artillery were overcome by Métis snipers from the woods, and they retreated after a day's fighting and eight casualties.

A number of Natives were about to ride off in pursuit of the retreating soldiers, but Poundmaker would not allow it. He said it was enough to have beaten off the enemy; it was good to have defended their families, but of taking the offensive he did not approve.

Riel now knew the Natives would never join him in rebellion. He became more delusional than ever. While Dumont was holding off Middleton's men at Fish Creek, Riel was busy making plans to move the Holy Roman Empire to Montreal and appoint a new pope. He began having visions again.

Then Dumont pulled back, luring Middleton's 800 men to Batoche where they spent three days firing away at an enemy they couldn't see because the Métis were, as usual, hidden in the bush. The militia, needless to say, suffered more casualties.

On the fourth day Middleton tried another attack, moving in on the Métis from two sides at once. This too failed, because the untrained militia missed their cues, and another day ended in disaster.

By this time Middleton was fed up with his soldiers, and they too, probably, with him. Ignoring his orders, the troops rode straight at the Métis, overwhelming them and killing twelve. The rest fled into the woods. When the Canadian scouts rode after them they found Gabriel Dumont, who told them he had ninety cartridges left for anyone who wanted to capture him. He was then left alone, and he too fled.

Some days later a party of scouts found Riel looking cold and disoriented. As one NWMP scout said, "His eyes rolled from side to side with the look of a hunted man." Riel surrendered and Middleton telegraphed to Macdonald:

"Riel is my prisoner. What is to be done with him? I await instructions." Riel was taken to a temporary jail in Regina. And with that the rebellion was over.

A Metis jacket, probably worn by Riel

Middleton's troops on a train to Fort Qu'Appelle

XLV
The End of the Line

The rebellion was over. Now came the trial.

Riel himself wanted to be tried by the Supreme Court. Orangemen wanted him hanged for treason and the murder of Thomas Scott: in life Scott was not a nice person, but passing years had made him a martyr and a hero. In Quebec sympathy was building for Riel, who was seen as a champion of the rights of Catholics and French speakers in the west.

The outcome of the trial hinged on whether or not Riel was sane.

It was decided to hold the trial in Regina, headquarters of the NWMP, where the judge (who was also the local magistrate) chose the jury by putting the names of thirty-six people he knew into a jar, shaking it up, and picking six. Not one of the six was Catholic or French-speaking.

The trial began on a hot day in the middle of July, 1885. Riel pleaded "not guilty". The Crown began by producing evidence of high treason, proof that Riel had waged war against the government. This was a letter that Riel had sent to the NWMP, demanding the surrender of Fort Carlton and threatening a "war of extermination". The Defence, in their turn, tried to prove that Riel was insane and delusional, and that the letter was not a real military threat.

The legal definition of insanity was that the accused person did not know right from wrong at the time when the crime was committed. The Defence called to the stand doctors who had treated Riel in various asylums. One of them objected to the legal definition as being unscientific. "It is all nonsense", he said, "to talk about a man not knowing what he is doing simply because he is insane....Dozens in the Toronto Asylum know right and wrong...and yet they are undoubtedly insane." General Middleton, amongst others, testified that Riel *did* know right from wrong.

Riel himself did not want to be seen as insane—that would lessen his credibility as a prophet of the new world: "I cannot fulfill my mission if I am looked upon as an insane being," he said. "Through the grace of God I am the founder of Manitoba."

The trial lasted for four days. At the end of it the jury were out less than an hour before returning a verdict of guilty (although they asked the judge for mercy, that is, a prison sentence rather than the death penalty). The judge nevertheless sentenced Riel to hang.

In Ontario the verdict was seen as fair and satisfactory; in Quebec Riel was seen as a martyr to the French cause, (which gave rise to a new Political party, the Parti National). The country was in an uproar, split into opposing camps—and to one degree or another has been ever since. The insanity defence controversy continues to this day: Was Riel sane or insane? Was he a criminal or a hero? Was he a traitor or the Father of Manitoba"? (Or, as Riel himself would have it, a Father of Confederation".)

While the trial of Riel was dividing the country, the CPR was busy uniting it. The final and most difficult section of the line was being built, through the Rockies. The engineer, Albert Bowman Rogers, chose the routes—Eagle Pass through the Monashee range, and through the Selkirk range a route later named for him, Rogers Pass. This was a winding, daring route built nearly 2000 feet above the Columbia River. The laying of track was delayed by avalanches, collapsed bridges, clay that was too soft to support track, and huge snowfalls. Hundreds of men died, among them some of the Chinese who had come over to work on the railroad.

At the same time the CPR again came close to bankruptcy. George Stephen again asked the government for a loan, and after much debate the Conservative majority in the House of Commons decided to lend the CPR more money.

So it came about that on November 7th, 1885, at Craigellachie in the Eagle Pass, the last spike was driven into the Canadian Pacific Railroad—one of the greatest engineering feats in the history of the world. The spike was driven, as seen in the famous photo, by Donald Smith—the silent partner and Macdonald's hated foe. The spike itself was not a purely ceremonial, flashy gold one, but a good, solid iron one like all the others.

On November 16th, in Regina, nine days after the completion of the railroad, Riel, carrying a small ivory crucifix, was led from his cell to the gallows by North West Mounted Policemen in their red tunics, and two priests. He was hanged before four witnesses, and early in December his body was returned to Red River on board a CPR train. He was buried at the cathedral in Saint Boniface.

Eleven days after Riel's execution, on November 27th, eight natives were hanged for murders they had committed during the rebellion. The eight included six Cree (Wandering Spirit, Miserable Man, Bad Arrow, Round the Sky, Iron Body and Little Bear) and two Assiniboine (Ikteh and Man Without Blood). They went to the gallows singing their death songs.

A Cree chief, Foremost Man, later sang a lament: "Where are the buffalo? Where are our horses? They are gone and we must follow them.... Give us the prairies again and we won't ask for food. But it is too late. It is too late; it is too late."

A curved railway bridge - moving west!

A new railway bridge

Building a snowshed over the track in the Rockies

XLVI
Last of the Titans

On June 28th, 1886, the first CPR transcontinental train left Montreal, to arrive at Vancouver six days later. On board was John A. Macdonald, seeing the west for the first time, through a luxury car window. Along the way he stopped here and there to campaign—an election was to be in a few months—and in the foothills he met with Crowfoot. They spoke of the chiefs who were serving three-year prison sentences for their part in the rebellion, Big Bear and Poundmaker. Crowfoot was Poundmaker's adoptive father and fear ed his son would die in prison. Crowfoot told this to Macdonald and the prime minister agreed to release Poundmaker. Big Bear was also later released after serving only part of his sentence.

On an April afternoon some four years later, Crowfoot, surrounded by friends and his last living relatives, lay dying in his tent near what is now Gleichen, Alberta.

"A little while and I will be gone from among you", he said to them. "From nowhere we came; into nowhere we go. What is life? It is the flash of a firefly in the night. It is the breath of a buffalo in winter time. It is the little shadow that moves across the grass and loses itself in the sunset."

Father Lacombe wrote a long obituary in the Macleod Gazette. At the end of it he wrote, "He is no more. No one like him will fill his place."

Macdonald went on to win a majority in that 1887 election. Four years later, in 1891, he suffered a stroke and died a week later on June 6th. His French colleague, Hector Langevin, was to give the eulogy in the House of Commons, but was so sad that he could not go on. "Mr. Speaker", he said, "I would have wished to ...speak of our dear, departed friend...and the goodness of his heart...but I feel that I must stop; my heart is full of tears. I cannot proceed further."

Huge crowds gathered along the route of the funeral procession in Ottawa. Macdonald's body was put on a CPR train draped in black and carried to Kingston, to be buried near other members of his family, including his parents, his first wife, and a child who had died many years ago.

Kind, warm-hearted, stubborn, noble, funny, articulate, intemperate, entertaining—lovable and very human—the first Prime Minister of Canada was all these things. There would be other prime ministers before the end of the 19th century, but the great achievements were Macdonald's. He had done the unlikely and the seemingly impossible: he had brought into being a nation, despite historical tensions and hostilities, with two languages and two religions; and he had managed to build the world's longest railway making it all possible, and for the first time connecting the Atlantic and Pacific shores of Canada. In addition, the British government in 1880 transferred to Canada all the Arctic Islands adjacent to its northern territories, reaching all the way to the seas around the North Pole. Canada's claim to sovereignty was later assured by the presence of an RCMP post established at Herschel Island in 1903.

Macdonald did not live to see it, but twenty years after the completion of the transcontinental railroad, part of the old North West Territories, formerly Rupert's Land, became the provinces of Alberta and Saskatchewan, joining Confederation in 1905. Still later, in 1912, the Hudson's Bay Company gave the territory known as Ungava to Quebec. the Canadian Government then designating it as a "Province in good standing".

And so was forged at last an unbroken chain of provinces, bordering the United States, and reaching all the way from the east to the west coast of the continent. and north almost to the Pole. Macdonald's vision had become reality. The country that had its beginnings nearly a thousand years before in Newfoundland had reached completion on the shores of the Pacific. After an immensely long and heroic journey through time and space, through an unimaginable wilderness of frozen tundra, forest, fly-infested lakes, vast plains, rock and water, a nation—forty times the size of the Mother Country—was formed. It would eventually cover 10 provinces, 3 Territories, 6 time zones, and many geographic and climate zones, reaching far up into the Arctic Ocean. We can recognize it as the Canada we know today: our Dominion, stretching from sea to sea – to sea.

And that's how Canada came to be.

J.A. MacDonald in old age

Ice floes on the Arctic Ocean

Furthest West - a BC beach near the Queen Charlotte Islands (Haida Gwai)